Tortillas

Tortillas

A CULTURAL HISTORY

• • • • •

Paula E. Morton

University of New Mexico Press • Albuquerque

Published 2014
Printed in the United States of America
19 18 17 16 15 14   1 2 3 4 5 6

Library of Congress Cataloging-in-Publication Data

Morton, Paula E.
  Tortillas : a cultural history / Paula E. Morton.
     pages cm
  Includes bibliographical references and index.
  ISBN 978-0-8263-5214-9 (pbk. : alk. paper)
  ISBN 978-0-8263-5215-6 (electronic)
  1. Tortillas—History. 2. Food habits—Mexico.
  3. Food habits—United States. I. Title.
  TX770.T65M67 2014
  641.81'5—dc23
                                        2014001976

Designed by Lisa Tremaine
Composed in Joanna and Monotype Gill

Cover art: La Tortillera, Diego Rivera, courtesy University of California,
San Francisco School of Medicine, San Francisco General Hospital
© 2014 Banco de México Diego Rivera Frida Kahlo Museums Trust, Mexico,
D.F. / Artists Rights Society (ARS), New York

For Niamh, Finnbar, Aife, Kevin, Allison, and Sarah,
who love a good tortilla

Contents

Preface

In the late 1990s I worked one day as a temp employee in an immigrant neighborhood tortillería, bordered to the south by the village of Anapra, Mexico; to the east, El Paso, Texas. I moved to New Mexico from a farm in Pennsylvania, and the most I knew about tortillas is that they tasted good in Pennsylvania and best at the borderlands, handmade and warm off the griddle. But this is not a book about my one-day-for-cheap-pay in a tortilla-making shop. I was curious. Who made the first tortilla? Where did the tortilla come from? What is an "authentic" traditional tortilla? This is a book about the history of the tortilla, from its roots in ancient Mesoamerica to the cross-cultural global tortilla. Though my sources are listed throughout the book and the bibliographic essay, I am especially indebted to the individuals who aided me with their knowledge and suggestions.

To the librarians and archivists, especially: Margarita Vargas-Betancourt, Paul Losch, and Richard Phillips, Latin American Collection, University of Florida; Michael Hironymous, Benson Latin American Collection, University of Texas at Austin; Elizabeth Flores, New Mexico State University; Elayne Silversmith, Smitsonian National Museum of the American Indian; Patricia Worthington, El Paso County Historical Society; Eloisa Levario, San Elizario Genealogy and Historical Society; Juli McLoone, University of Texas at San Antonio; Jannelle Weakly, Arizona State Museum; Jeannette Garcia, Tohono O'odham Nation Cultural Center and Museum; and Tammy Popejoy, American Institute of Baking (AIB International).

To the historians, food scientists, anthropologists, and those who shared your expertise, specifically: Maribel Alvarez, Margaret Beck, Frances Berdan, David Cheetham, George Cowgill, Michael Dunn, Ronald Faulseit, Gary Feinman, Richard Ford, David Grove, Kimberly Heinle, Laura Kosakowsky, Susan Milbrath, Barbara Mills, Mary Paganelli, Tony Payan, Karina Jazmín Juárez Ramírez, Lloyd Rooney, Alan Sandstrom, Sergio Serna-Saldivar, John Staller, Barbara Stark, Dan Strehl, and CiCi Williamson.

To Minsa Corn Flour Inc. and Rodrigo Ariceaga and David Herrera, for your on-site introduction to the tortilla production business.

To Jim Kabbani, Tortilla Industry Association, and Dave Waters, Lawrence Equipment.

To Gruma Corporation and Miguel Arce Monroy for documents and video about Gruma.

To the tortilla makers for your good food and good conversation: Ana Baca, Rodolfo Gamez, Louis Guerra, Joel Leal, Fernando Luna Jr., Shauna Page, José Rubio Jr., Fernando Ruiz, Mercedes Secundino, and José Solis.

To the home cooks: Eva Ybarra, María Baron, and Yvonne Tarin. To the professional chefs: Pilar Cabrera and her assistant Saskia Fiselier, and Pati Jinich.

To my borderland friends in Arizona, New Mexico, Texas, and Mexico, especially: Maribel Alvarez, Carlos Angulo, Howard Campbell, Mary Carter at the Women's Intercultural Center, Aurora Dawson, Jaime Garcia, Moira Murphy, Tony Payan, Sandra Rodriguez, Gustavo de la Rosa, Graciela de la Rosa, Sister Silvia, Dorothy Truax, Lillian Trujillo, and Lucinda Vargas. To Mario Dena and Adriana Barradas for your tour of a maquila in Ciudad Juárez, Mexico.

To Enrique Gaytán Cortázar, Agregado Cultural at the Consulado General de México in El Paso, Texas, for your enlightened conversations. Thank you for contributing your poem, "Undocumented."

To Alberto Fierro, Consul de México, Orlando, Florida, for your introduction to Odilon Mezquite, Israel Secundino, Lourdes Mayorga, and the local Mexican-American community.

To the individuals for your tortilla stories: Rabbi Arnold Mark Belzer, Joe Bravo, Jordan Buckley, Miguel González, Nezahualcoyotl Xiuhtecutli (Neza), Leonel Pérez, Margarita Vargas-Betancourt, and Eva Ybarra.

To Tom Wilbur, photographer, for transforming illustrations into the correct resolution for publication, and your talented map-drawing.

To Ramses Omar Cabrales, for donating your time to translate Spanish documents and email messages.

To Alonso Ortiz Galan, National Council for Cultural Arts, Mexico (Conaculta), for your exceptional research assistance in Mexico.

To John Byram, director at the University of New Mexico Press, an excellent editor. Thank you for your interest and encouragement. To Linda Kay Norris, copyeditor, for your worthy contributions to this endeavor.

To my family, for your support, laughter, and love: my husband Barry; Jessica and Paul Ruane and their family, Niamh, Finnbar, and Aife; Bridget and Joseph Nastasi and their family, Kevin, Sarah, and Allison. You are always there for me.

Prologue

• • • THE HUMBLE TORTILLA

The history of the tortilla is a tale of the powerful intersections of people, customs, and culinary traditions that continues to lift generations and cultures. Two years ago I interviewed Eva Ybarra at her home in Anthony, New Mexico, halfway between Las Cruces, New Mexico, and El Paso, Texas. Trying to avoid the stifling heat of the day by working in the shadow of her mobile home, Eva patted round tortillas from corn dough and flipped them, no more than thirty seconds on each side, on the cast-iron griddle heated on a backyard grill. We ate tacos made from melt-in-your-mouth tortillas and talked about her life in Mexico and the United States. Her story of the tortilla as the "bread of life" is a reflection of the connections between Mesoamericans around 2,500 years ago and today's international tortilla marketplace.

"When you are hungry, pray you have tortillas." As a child living in an isolated settlement of farm worker families in the Chihuahua high desert of northern Mexico, Eva learned there were winter days between harvests when there was nothing to eat except tortillas. No beans. No squash. Only tortillas imbued with the sweet flavor of fresh ground corn infused with mineral lime. In their tiny kitchen space, her mother flattened little balls of moist corn dough called *masa* between her hands, patted the dough into thin disks, and briefly cooked the thin disks on the comal, the hot clay griddle coated with lime to prevent sticking. She knew precisely when to remove the tortillas, puffy as the moisture inside was released from the dough. In the center of the table she placed the basket piled with warm, soft tortillas wrapped in an embroidered cloth, and a bowl of spicy pulverized chiles mixed with water. Eva used the tortilla rolled in the Mexican way as a spoon. She then "*churrito-ed*" it between her hands with a little salt scratched on the warm tortilla to make a funnel-type cake.

It was the 1950s and the Mexican Miracle stimulating economic growth with urban industrial development and large-scale modern agriculture production did not reach Eva's family. The "miracle" pretty much expired by the time it reached the powerless rural poor. While Elvis Presley topped the music charts with "Heartbreak Hotel" and the television sitcom family of Ozzie and Harriet idealized suburban California upright family life, Eva's father focused on earning enough money to buy corn to grind for the daily batch of tortillas.

They could do without store-bought shoes but not without tortillas. Tortillas prepared from ground corn soaked in mineral lime almost doubled the available protein and amino acids in corn. Tortillas satisfied hunger pangs, and paired with beans and chile sauce they provided the nutrition and calories to make it through a day of hard work. Corn was inexpensive, easy to grow, and converting corn into tortillas was part of the education of every woman in rural Mexico. But more than a necessity, tortillas were a choice for Eva's family, their Mexican identity linked with this ancient Mesoamerican food.

Eva's father grew up poor in Mexico, the son of a farm laborer. He was landless, poorly educated, and poorly paid, yet confident, strong, and determined. With his copper skin, dark eyes, dark hair, broad brow, and prominent nose he looked every bit of his indigenous heritage, a striking contrast to his wife descended from a mestizo hybrid of colonial Spanish and native Indio. "She was light with blue eyes . . . so beautiful," says Eva.

In Mexico it mattered that Eva's mother passed as the socially acceptable Spanish and her grandparents owned a house and cows. Ever since the Spaniards conquered the Aztec in 1521 there were issues between indigenous and Spanish heritage, brown skin and light complexion, land poor and landowner, people of corn and people of wheat. Eva's father had a lot of convincing to do.

"Theirs was a love story," says Eva. Her mother, paralyzed in one leg, probably from polio, was not able to dance. At the time young men courted eligible women at public dances, for a respectable unmarried woman did not go out alone on a date. Eva's father brought the dance to her house, hiring the dance musicians to serenade her, and she melted. "How will you support her?" her parents asked. "I have two hands to work and will help her as much as I can in the home," he said. And so they married and he fulfilled his promise, working in the fields all day and coming home in the evening to hang laundry or grind corn for tortillas.

Eva's father's participation in the making of tortillas was a rarity. The traditional division of labor among the close-knit farming community was clear: men planted and harvested the corn, and women shelled, soaked, rinsed, and ground the corn to produce the dough formed into round tortillas—an arduous job requiring at least six hours a day. Even after the 1920s, when more and more villages in rural Mexico supported their own molino de nixtamal, the cornmill powered by electric, steam, or gasoline, it was men's work to hold the position of miller and operate the machinery. Women's work was to prepare the corn for grinding the traditional way, carry it in pails to the mill, and wait in line for the corn to be ground. In some instances, such as in remote Tepoztlán, Mexico, during the early 1940s, as anthropologist Oscar Lewis observed: "for a man to be seen carrying corn to the mill is a great humiliation."

When Eva's family shared tortillas at the dinner table, they did not talk about the culture of the tortilla, its Mesoamerican roots, or the role of the tortilla in politics and the economy. They were there to eat and love tortillas. "Warm, soft, fresh from the griddle heated on the wood stove. Or if we were lucky, a little cheese or beef folded into a taco. Stale tortillas, we cut into pieces and fried," Eva remembers. "We never wasted a bit of a tortilla."

"My brother remembers there was only enough corn for tortillas twice a day instead of three times." It was the time of the tortilla crisis in Mexico when the corn crop failed. The government-supported expansion of export wheat at the expense of corn production set the stage for shortages and price increases. "In Guanajuato people stood in line all night in the hopes of getting a handful of maize for the day's tortillas," notes historian Enrique Ochoa.

On the farm her father's wages were cut. He listened to the stories of his neighbors who headed north across the border to work. He noticed bags of corn and beans and the precious backyard pig bought with dollars sent back home. In 1947, desperate for a way to feed and clothe his family, he signed up to leave his country.

Eva is the daughter of a bracero, her father a Mexican guest worker recruited to the United States in the 1940s and then returned to Mexico in the '50s. "Renting Mexicans" is how historian Rodolfo Acuña describes the process. The bracero labor program represented a contractual agreement between the Mexican and U.S. governments, originally conceived to alleviate World War II labor shortages in the U.S. Between 1942 and 1964 when the Bracero Program ended, a surge of more than four million braceros came to work temporarily in the U.S. on contract to growers and ranchers.

Vaccinated, blood tested, deloused, and ID'd, Eva's father landed in Mesilla Valley, New Mexico, bordered on the south by Mexico and on the east by Texas. There he picked cotton and weeded chile fields for a minimum wage of about thirty cents an hour plus transportation to and from the U.S. and farm worker housing. He saved his family from starving. In return, the growers gained hard-working labor for a nasty, physically demanding job no one wanted.

Eva was almost born in the United States, but by 1953 her father's contract expired and the official bracero program began to unravel. On paper it looked as if the agreement provided something for everyone. Yet within a few years U.S. local labor opposed imported workers and the Mexican government complained about the treatment of their guest workers. Farm wages dropped and agriculture adopted laborsaving technology. Ultimately, the governments terminated the program in 1964, too late to halt the flow of Mexicans, documented and undocumented, who continued to cross the border and disperse into communities through the United States.

Why not remain in New Mexico and live and work beneath the radar of the immigration officials? Two of Eva's sisters were U.S. citizens, born in New Mexico. Other bracero families stayed put in their new communities despite daunting arrests of undocumented immigrants and deportations. But Mexico was home. Mexico was family.

"I was born in our old house, empty for almost eight years," says Eva. Her parents returned to their home at the base of arid foothills on La Laguna Rancho where the landowner raised cattle and grew crops irrigated by the Rio Conchos, a tributary of the Rio Grande in the state of Chihuahua. Shade cottonwoods grew along the riverbed, but much of the surrounding land around the settlement was shrub desert dotted with thorny mesquite, cacti, and succulent plants able to withstand months of intense heat, drought, and cold desert winds.

On the steep hillside rising above the desert floor in the shallow depressions where rainwater collected, at the end of the workday the farm laborers planted small communal plots of corn on eroded land in soil depleted of nutrients. "Only water from God," explains Eva. If the fickle summer monsoon season produced sufficient rain for the corn to tassel, the kernels matured. The ripe ears of corn dried on the stalk, then were harvested and stored until ground into corn dough for tortillas.

No rain, no harvest, and the family squeezed a bit more from the budget to buy corn.

It was easy for Eva's family to resume housekeeping. They opened the unlocked door to their two-room adobe cottage built from dried clay, swept the pressed dirt floor, brushed the spider webs from the latrine out back, stoked the wood stove, added kerosene to the lamp, and carried their wooden table and chairs into the kitchen and a three-drawer chest with a mirror to the bedroom. In one section of the kitchen Eva's father constructed a handmade plank bin, ready to store their corn supply through the winter. Corn was as protected as jewelry kept in a jewelry box.

From old Mexico to New Mexico and again back to Mexico, Eva's mother packed and unpacked her tortilla-making tools— the three-legged metate, a sloping oblong stone to grind corn, and the mano, a cylinder hand-held stone rolled on the metate to crush the kernels. The metate was rock heavy, made from volcanic basalt, solid, and cured from use, intended to last generations unless dropped and broken, and then there would be tears and recrimination. To make chile sauce her mother tossed a handful of chiles into the molcajete, a thick bowl of porous volcanic rock also supported by three short legs, then pulverized the skins and seeds with a pestle called a tejolote. The comal, the clay griddle, was reserved in its place of honor on top of the wood-burning stove.

Eva's mother made tortillas the traditional way. Each evening she poured their daily supply of corn kernels into a large pot of boiling water, lowered the heat, and added a couple of spoonfuls of mineral lime powder obtained from builders lime— processed lime produced from baked limestone ground into a powder. "We called it cal, the same cal used to paint white every house in the village," says Eva. "The next morning we carried the pot of steeped corn to the river behind our house and rinsed and rubbed the softened skins." The tough outer covering eventually peeled off the kernels.

Perhaps as a side remark, Eva's mother mentioned that the ancient Indios made tortillas this way, but she knew the unique food preparation process called *nixtamalization* as simply "natural made" tortillas. She was always careful not to include too much mineral lime, because it would make the dough yellow and taste bitter, and careful not to burn the tortillas on the griddle, because it brought bad luck to the household.

When Eva's father came home from working in the fields, he ground the soaked and softened corn in the brown desert yard. Outside the kitchen door under a lean-to roof he fastened a manual grinding mill to a post. The grinding was slow going and required a well-muscled arm. There was no mechanized corn dough mill in the area, but even if there had been, the cost to take their corn to the mill was prohibitive. "My mother reground the corn on the metate but only a short time to give it the corn flavor from the porous grinding stone," says Eva. "She was particular about her tortilla dough."

The contrast between the lifestyle of the urban working class and the average rural laborer was significant. Eva's family had no electricity, gas stove, running water, or indoor plumbing. As an unskilled farm laborer on a mechanized farm, her father cleaned debris from irrigation ditches or mended fences to earn a paltry income. In a good year when corn yields were high he bought cull corn directly from the fields at a discount. In a poor year his family was hungry.

If Eva's family had lived in the city, electricity and modern appliances like the electric corn grinder would have made life easier. Electricity also drew factories into the city, supplying desperately needed jobs. In the city low-income women walked to the corner State Food Agency store and bought a bag of dehydrated nixtamal corn flour, an innovative method to prepare tortillas by adding water to processed corn flour. Instant tortillas were an easy solution to feed the poor, said the politicians and industrialists. The women responsible for feeding their families

Eva Ybarra makes home-
made tortillas prepared
from corn ground on the
traditional metate and
mano, Anthony, New
Mexico, 2012. (Courtesy
of Yvonne Tarin)

sacrificed tradition and the taste of fresh lime-soaked corn for a
dependable supply of affordable tortillas. But electricity, industrial jobs, State Food stores, and instant corn flour migrated from
the city to the country very slowly. Eva's father could not wait.

During those years in La Laguna Rancho, Eva's father did not
get ahead. He went on with his life, often gone for days, hiring
himself out to farms a distance from his home. By the mid-1960s
Mexico's economic growth leveled off while the nation's population grew and urbanization accelerated. Wide economic and
social gaps separated the urban and rural areas, the wealthy and
the poor, the skilled and unskilled.

It did not take long for Eva's father to notice he earned less and
less and competed with an excess of farm workers with mar-
ginal skills. Eva's mother paid more at the store. Eva wished for
wheat flour tortillas. At Christmas time the landowner's daughter ate large, thick flour tortillas made from wheat harvested
from a field reserved for the owner's personal use and ground

into smooth, fine flour at the mill. "Flour tortillas were a big deal," Eva says.

In the end, Eva's father decided to return to New Mexico. Pulling up roots again beat food insecurity. They lived one year in Ciudad Juárez, Mexico, across the river from El Paso, Texas, waiting for their papers, official documents so they could cross the border legally over the international bridge and did not have to swim across the Rio Grande at night in between the U.S. Border Patrol lookouts. One of her older sisters remained in their village in Mexico, but today Eva is afraid for her sister's safety. Although the town is not on the main route for drug trafficking, turf battles between cartels intrude into their quiet life.

In 1970, Eva and her family moved to Mesquite, New Mexico, in the Rio Grande Valley outside Las Cruces. This relocation produced much the same routine for Eva's father: picking corn, cotton, and chiles. But Eva's mother adjusted her tortilla tradition. In the early morning she mixed lard and water with store-bought packaged wheat flour and stretched or rolled the dough into thick flour tortillas. Heated and filled with beans or meat, chile, and cheese, the hefty, portable burritos fed the farm workers. In the evening she made the usual corn tortillas for her family, in part because this was what she knew but also because the overflowing stuffed flour burrito was an American luxury.

Today, Eva is married and lives close to the border of Mexico on the United States side in the small, close-knit working-class town of Anthony, New Mexico, where Spanish is spoken as often as English and Lady of Guadalupe shrines protect the home. Eva preserves her mother's metate and mano as family heirlooms, always present, and buys tortillas machine-made from masa harina, dried and powdered corn flour, at the local supermarket's in-store tortillería, the fast-food component of inexpensive, quick, and convenient tortillas in the borderlands.

On special occasions Eva gets together with her daughter Yvonne and friend María from Mexico. They make tortillas the

Enrique's homemade
mechanical corn grinder,
Anthony, New Mexico,
2012.

traditional way, although they buy field corn already shelled from
the local farm supply store. They soak the kernels overnight in the
alkaline solution of limewater, rinse the corn to remove the outer
skin, and transport it to Enrique, who lives a few blocks from Eva.
Enrique is a bracero child born in Tempe, Arizona, and raised
in Chihuahua, Mexico. Eighty-seven years old, Enrique grinds
corn for people in the community who appreciate nixtamal corn
dough. He reconstructed two unsatisfactory electric corn grinders
from Juárez, Mexico, into one good machine that grinds seventy
pounds of corn in twenty minutes. In a small enclosed space off
the kitchen, Enrique feeds batches of the wet corn into the mouth
of the grinder until the output reaches the desired consistency of
fine ground masa, the corn dough that makes the best tortillas.

Eva pays him eight dollars and returns home with the masa
to pat into tortillas. For Eva the exciting part about making tortillas is what happens when she is back in her kitchen, where she

chooses what to fold into the tortilla and which chiles bursting with capsaicin to prepare for the dipping sauce. The versatile tortilla is never boring.

Enrique says his customers think fresh ground corn tortillas taste like home. Eva says the smell of the lime-soaked corn reminds her of her father grinding corn in their backyard with his hand grinder and her mother cooking tortillas on the wood stove. "Tortillas are family ties, my mother's devotion, and being Mexican," she says. It is understood that tortillas do not need symbolic rituals or corn ceremonies to preserve the tradition handed down through the generations.

Yet traditions evolve to represent the world's diversity and modernization. People migrate, cultures blend, and the production and marketing of tortillas change. What is the significance of the ancient Mesoamerican tortilla tradition? Hand-patted disks of fresh masa tortillas from a taco truck in Los Angeles, California, are not the same as the "Gringo Special" in the Tex-Mex Taco Bar in Stockholm, Sweden. Tortillas are everywhere. How did the traditional handmade tortilla morph into one of the most dynamic mass-produced world foods? How will the traditional tortilla survive as it confronts its modern role as an international cross-cultural food star?

Chapter 1

• • • THE INCOMPARABLE TORTILLA

Deep in the highlands of Chiapas in southeastern Mexico, a contemporary Zinacantecos shaman kneels before three wooden crosses decorated with pine tree tops and bunches of red geraniums. As he prays to his ancestral Maya gods who reside inside the volcanic mountains, the shaman plants white wax candles in the earth before the shrine, waves copal incense over the lighted candles, and pours a powerful brew of cane liquor on the ground. For the ceremonial smoke, he lights cigarettes in the guise of burning incense. And he presents corn tortillas, the life-giver, to eat, perceived in the image of the flaming candles as the heat energy of the sun released into the soil to grow the sacred corn. "The gods' meals are like those eaten by men. Or, as the Zinacantecos express it, men eat what the gods eat," explained anthropologist Evon Vogt. Fed and contented, the gods are ready to talk and the Zinacantecos listen to their ancestors, spiritual counselors who provide order to a world of crop failures, squabbling relatives, and modernization.

More than two thousand miles northwest of the mountain shrine, Joe Bravo, a Chicano artist, pays tribute to his Hispanic heritage in his backyard studio in Los Angeles, California. He paints on a twenty-seven-inch wheat flour tortilla, custom made by a local tortillería. The ritual begins with selecting the desired texture, shape, and color of the tortilla and cooking it over an open flame. Burn marks are a distinctive characteristic. With bold acrylics he paints an ethnic Elvis Presley with a dark Latino complexion, a snake entwined Medusa or Our Lady of Guadalupe, Patron Saint of Mexico. Bravo's canvas is at the mercy of the elements, and after the paint dries he protects it against moisture and

La Virgin of Guadalupe. *Tortilla Art by Joe Bravo.* (Courtesy of Joe Bravo)

insects with an acrylic varnish. He grew up eating tortillas: "As the tortillas have given us life, I give it new life by using it as an art medium."

Our Story Begins in Mesoamerica

How did this seemingly humble food become such a venerated object of modern ritual and art? The rich cultural story of the tortilla begins its narrative in ancient Mesoamerica, a cultural and economic region extending from present day Central Mexico to Belize, Guatemala, El Salvador, Honduras, Nicaragua, and Costa Rica. The influence of this region also stretched into southeastern Central America, northwestern and northeastern Mexico, and what is now the southwestern United States. In the highlands—the Central Valley of Mexico, the mountainous region of Oaxaca, and the intermountain basins of Chiapas and Guatemala—the people terraced and irrigated the agricultural triad of corn, beans, and squash; mined gold, silver, and obsidian; and ruled from powerful urban metropolises. In the lowlands—the eastern coasts of the Gulf of Mexico and the Caribbean, and the western Pacific coast—the native people added chiles and tobacco to the triad, planted cacao trees, extracted salt from the earth, and built scattered rural centers of political authority. The geography was as varied as its ethnic populations and provided the basis for the tortilla's culinary and cultural diversity.

Ambitious politicians and priests established the basic Mesoamerican pattern of the community. Rulers administrated, priests celebrated, warriors fought, long-haul merchants traded, and peasants labored to build temples and palaces and grow food.

In the southern lowlands of Veracruz, Mexico, and the neighboring state of Tabasco, from 1200–400 BC the hereditary elite class of the Olmec, acknowledged as the Mother Culture of Mexico, pronounced the rules of their land. They performed religious rituals in the shadow of ceremonial mounds and pyramids constructed out of clay and earth. They carved colossal heads out of volcanic basalt, some over nine feet high, of their

Mesoamerica map. (Tom Wilbur; redrawn from *Map of Mesoamerica*, Foundation for the Advancement of Mesoamerican Studies)

mighty kings and gods. Since there were no draft horses, cattle, or wagons before the Spanish conquest, the workers hauled tons of basalt by hand from a distance of more than fifty miles to the capital San Lorenzo Tenochtitlán.

In the highlands of the Valley of Oaxaca, Mexico, Mesoamerican glyphs appeared in a pictorial form of signs and a common number system. As early as 500 BC, Zapotec priests described their ceremonies in incipient forms of writing on the stone edifices of temples built 1,300 feet above the plain in the capital of Monte Albán. Below, the lowly laboring subjects in the fields looked up at the stone and mortar of the ruling class.

In the lowlands of Petén, Guatemala, at the capital of El Mirador in the height of its power between 300–150 BC, the Maya reached to the sky to praise their deities. Faced with cut stone and decorated with stucco masks of the gods and goddesses, the Danta Pyramid soared 270 feet high, as tall as an eighteen-story building. Its companion pyramid, Tigre, topped at 180 feet.

Major city-states emerged. In the Valley of Mexico over one hundred thousand people resided in the city of Teotihuacán, which spread over eight perfectly surveyed square miles with wide streets laid out on a grid plan, central markets, and three grand pyramids, the Pyramid of the Sun, the Pyramid of the Moon, and at the southern end of the Avenue of the Dead, the Temple of Quetzalcóatl. Over time, between AD 200–700, Teotihuacán became one of the largest cities in the world. Yet by AD 900 most of the great Classic city-states were abandoned, leaving unanswered questions to explain their collapse.

The people of Mesoamerica did regroup. After AD 950 regional commercial governments emphasized grand houses and royal feasts, art and science, and military and economic alliances. In the Mexican Yucatán, the elite class of Maya astronomers surveyed the sun, moon, and planets from the platforms and windows of the ornate stone carved Caracol observatory at the urban center of Chichen Itza. In Central Mexico in 1325, the Mexica, the most dominant of the seven Aztec tribes, founded the lake island city of Tenochtitlán, the site of present day Mexico City. In the center of their capital city they framed the political and religious complex of more than seventy-five formal structures around the Templo Mayor, the Great Temple, dedicated to two gods, Huitzilopochtli (God of War) and Tlaloc (God of Rain and Agriculture). The Aztec grew to form one of the most influential empires in Mesoamerican history until the arrival of the Spanish conquistadores in the sixteenth century.

Over three major time periods—the Preclassic, or Formative, from 1500 BC–AD 300, the Classic from AD 300–950, and the Postclassic from AD 950–1521—the complex histories of these civilizations are each rooted in the history of corn, a grain discovered, domesticated, and ritualized by the people throughout Mesoamerica.

Sin Maíz No Hay País

For the Mesoamericans, there was no country without corn, "*Sin maíz no hay país.*" For the Maya, the Aztec, the Zapotec, and the wide diversity of regional cultures from the nomadic people of the north to the southern periphery to the western frontier, corn was the equivalent of the staple European bread. In fact, in Old World Europe corn was the generic term for a variety of grains, such as wheat and rice and barley. Maize was a New World name, believed to be a variant of the word *mahiz* spoken by the indigenous Taíno people to an awed Christopher Columbus, who pulled back the leaves of the corn plant to reveal small white kernels.

But the Mesoamericans were not content with one name for this extraordinary grain that transformed the nomadic hunter and gatherer into the sedentary farmer and homemaker. In the Valley of Mexico the people called corn by its Nahuatl name *tlaolli* and changed labels to distinguish each stage of the corn plant's development. The tender and undeveloped ear was *xilot*; as it formed kernels, *elotl*; and the dried ear, *centli*.

Corn, related to wild primitive teosinte grass, was cultivated between 7500–5000 BC in Mexico and Central America. In the Guilá Naquitz cave near Mitla in the Valley of Mexico, archaeologists uncovered cob fragments dating to approximately 4300 BC. Initially the early foragers collected the primitive corn from the wild, but gradually they deliberately took a few of the largest and most flavorful seeds and planted them beside their dwellings, and now they produced a corn crop. But corn is wind pollinated, carried by the wind from the tassels (male) to the silks (female). Thus, distance, wind currents, and cross-contamination affected the pollination of corn, leading to a large number of corn varieties over thousands of years of selection.

Wherever they settled, whatever the climate or soil, the diverse people of Mesoamerica planted many varieties of corn and it grew. From season to season, the farmers saved seeds from the largest, most productive and hardy plants. With repeated selection, corn varieties developed for every need and every microclimate: the humid lowlands, the temperate mountain valleys, and the short rainfall seasons of the desert. One variety dyed maize beer a reddish color; the broad husks of another variety were used to wrap tamales. Starchy mature corn was preferred for tortillas.

The Mesoamericans prayed to gods and goddesses of rain and corn, talked to the tender shoots of corn, touched the moisture of the soil, and harvested the ears to nourish their bodies and souls. And some believed the first human beings were created from corn dough.

Corn Dough Beginnings

Consulting the *Popol Vuh*, the sacred Book of Counsel, the lords of the Quiché Maya of the Guatemalan highlands told the story of the first sunrise, the glories of the gods, and the rise of the maize deity, father of the mythical hero twins Hunahpú and Xbalanqué who crushed monsters and fought evil to make the world a decent place for humans. The human being was the next challenge for the gods.

After much deliberation, the forefather gods, Tepew and Q'ukumatz, formed figures from mud and wood, semblances of people but unable to walk or talk and, most important, pay homage to the gods. Stumped, the gods turned to Grandmother Xmucane at the high mountain named Split Place, Bitter Water Place. She picked up a jug and walked to the mountain stream where she mixed the clear water with kernels scraped from corn grown inside the sacred mountain. Then she knelt before the grinding stone to massage the corn into a coarse dough. Now the gods had the life force of corn to work with and they molded the dough into four men and four women made of flesh, perfect in their own image. And the gods were alarmed, for only gods were divine. So they blew a few puffs of fog in the eyes of the humans to remove the divine visionary power, leaving behind the wise guidance of the *Popol Vuh.*

Beyond the borders of the Maya, the Aztec spun their own legend of creation. The great cities of the Maya were in decline when the Aztec tribes immigrated to the Valley of Mexico.

Led by the deity Huitzilopochtli, they wandered south from the harsh desert of northern Mexico, a place they called the mythical Aztlán (Place of the White Heron). Along the arduous journey, they told and retold versions of their creation stories, where they came from and who they were as they made their way into an unknown world.

The Aztec paid homage to two primordial deities, Ometecuhtli, Lord of Duality, and Omecíhuatl, Lady of Duality, who delegated the monumental task of creating the world to their sons, Quetzalcóatl and Huitzilopochtli. These obedient sons made fire, sun, rain, rivers, mountains, plants, animals—a complete universe ruled by the gods. It only remained for the gods to create human beings.

Hero-god Quetzalcóatl, the feathered serpent, descended to the underworld of Mictlán to gather the bones and ashes of previous lost generations, intending to recreate humans from the bones of the spirits. The more bones he accumulated, the more he dropped and broke, and that is why, the Aztec legends said, some people are short, others tall. Undeterred by his less than perfect collection, Quetzalcóatl delivered his jumble to the earth fertility goddess Cihuacóatl-Quilaztli, the lady of the serpent skirt and necklace of human hearts. Cihuacóatl ground the sacred corn with the ancestral bones to make a dough, added a bit of sacrificial blood from Quetzalcóatl to fuel the creation, and after four days, created a male child followed in another four days by a female child.

Masa

The corn of the myths was good food, an important source of carbohydrates and protein. Early Mesoamericans chewed the entire ears—cob, husk, silk—of young tender corn, or roasted and boiled on the cob at its peak flavor. To grind corn into dough, the women crushed partially cooked and softened corn kernels between the mano, a hand stone that resembled a small elongated rolling-pin, and the metate, a slightly hollowed grinding stone carved from volcanic rock. The Aztec woman molded the ball of grainy dough in her hands and called it textli; the Maya called the dough yokem. The Spanish renamed it masa.

It was the woman's task to spend four or five hours a day on her knees grinding corn on the metate, similar to the concave grinding stone in ancient Egypt, and one of the oldest domestic tools in the Americas. She placed a small amount of prepared corn kernels on the metate, leaned over, and rolled the mano back and forth—three passes for a skilled grinder to partially grind for a corn drink. She repeated the sequence until she was satisfied with the texture to make tortillas and tamales. It was hard work bending and grinding, and in time she rubbed the palms of her hands raw, and the joints of her fingers ached. Naturally, the women who ground the corn expressed their

Metate and mano for grinding corn.

preference for enhanced efficiency and ease as the tool's design improved from the early basin metates shaped like a bowl, to the open end trough metates, to the most agreeable, the rectangular slab metate supported on three legs and sloped to facilitate grinding from high end to low end and catch the ground corn flour in a metate bin.

Once the Mesoamericans had the corn dough to work with, they added water and transformed it into a thick gruel called *atolli*. They concocted a fermented drink called *posolli* and prepared tamales, filled or plain, wrapped in banana leaves or corn husks and then steamed on hot coals. The tortilla we know today is a direct descendent of this same ancient corn dough.

Nixtamal: The Heart of the Traditional Corn Tortilla

Then there were the conscientious cooks, the women who simmered the hard kernels of mature corn in an alkali solution of mineral lime and water to make nixtamal corn, the heart of the traditional tortilla. Perhaps a woman accidently spilled ashes from the cooking fire into the pot filled with corn kernels and water and observed, yes, this corn cooked quicker than before, the kernels were easier to grind, and the corn dough stayed fresh longer. As the women talked together and experimented, someone stirred a scoop of powder from processed lime used to plaster homes into the water used to simmer and soak the kernels. Now the mineral lime improved the removal of the tough outer shell of the kernel, the pericarp, and lime replaced wood ashes as an ingredient. The Aztec called the washed, alkaline cooked corn nixtamalli from the Nahuatl words nextli (ashes) and tamalli (corn dough); the Spanish, nixtamal.

Mesoamericans obtained lime for the nixtamal solution from

Mexican Cookbook

"Mexican food has, ever since the 'American Occupation,' been a part of the Southwestern diet," wrote Erna Fergusson in *Mexican Cookbook*, published in 1945. The cooks in Fergusson's New Mexican community processed corn and prepared puffy corn tortillas "the old way," dating back to the time when the province of New Mexico was part of the Republic of Mexico. Fergusson added, "The only way to be sure of making tortillas correctly is to have a line of Indian ancestry running back about five hundred years." This recipe is courtesy of the University of New Mexico Press.

Corn: *Nixtamal* or Hominy

To Hull: 1 quart unslaked lye or wood ashes
           1 gallon water

Boil about half an hour, then stir until it stops bubbling. Strain and add as much shelled corn as the water will cover. Boil slowly until the hulls slip easily between the fingers. Pour into a colander to drain. Wash in several waters until the taste of lye is gone.

    This is the *nixtamal* that may be used fresh, dried for storing, or ground to make *masa*. Ideally corn should be prepared fresh for leachates of wood ashes, cremated marine and freshwater shells, or processed lime from the raw material. Regionally, families cut the soft limestone from outcrops of surface limestone rocks into chunks and cooked them over a hot fire in a kiln or oven for several days until the chemical composition changed to calcium oxide (CaO) and could be easily ground into a powder. Mixed with the proper proportions of water, the powder made a white plaster for coating walls or producing lime water for nixtamalization, a ratio worked out by the women to equal approximately 2.2 pounds of corn, 1 cup of water, and 1 tablespoon of the mineral lime.

The nutritional value of the mixture was unexpectedly enhanced because the lime infused masa (corn dough) increased

---

every dish, but as the recipes indicate, ready-ground corn meal may be substituted for *masa*.

The best corn meal is the blue corn meal now generally available. It is prepared by washing and sun-drying the kernels, roasting them in adobe ovens, and grinding. The meal ground on *metates* or in old-fashioned watermills seems to have a better flavor than the product of modern machinery. And who knows why?

· · · · ·

Tortillas (with corn meal)
2 cups corn meal or *masa*
1 teaspoon salt
warm water

Mix corn meal or *masa* and salt. If dry meal is used, add enough water to make a stiff dough, even the *masa* may require a little moisture. Adding 1 cup white flour to this recipe will make the dough easier to handle.

Set dough aside for 20 minutes, wet hands in water, mold balls of dough the size of hens' eggs, pat into thin cakes, and bake on soapstone or lightly greased griddle, turning until brown on both sides.

the human digestive system's ability to access niacin, six amino acids, and calcium. Over time the people who cooked corn in this alkali solution noticed they felt energized and healthy, and a food staple was born. "So superior is nixtamalized maize to the unprocessed kind that it is tempting to see the rise of Mesoamerican civilization as a consequence of this invention, without which the peoples of Mexico and their southern neighbors would have remained forever on the village level," argued anthropologist Sophie Coe. In fact, although the Europeans adopted corn as an important grain for feed and food, they largely ignored the nixtamal process, difficult to mill and prepare. As a result, poor people who depended on corn gruel without the nixtamal treatment for most of their energy suffered nutrition deficiencies like pellagra caused by a chronic lack of niacin (vitamin B_3).

The First Tortilla

Making tortillas was more complicated than simply stirring water into corn dough to make gruel. Tortillas required a source of mineral lime to soak and soften the small tough kernels of the early varieties of corn. At maturity, the kernels contained desired percentages of hard and soft starch. Tortillas required tortilla-making tools: a large cooking pot, a colander for rinsing, a metate and mano to grind the corn into the corn dough, and a flat griddle. Tortillas required fuel for a cooking fire, the technique to work the proper consistency of dough, and time for women to spend away from the fields to prepare ingredients and cook. So why create the tortilla?

The tortilla was a practical extension of the prevalent corn crop, an innovative dish to add to the repertoire of an extensive corn menu. The tortilla tasted delicious, combining it with beans and squash provided a trio of adequate nutrition, and folded it was a spoon. Merchants, traders, and specialized workers in the expanding city-states carried the stuffed tortilla to work. "Put simply, it is expedient and portable," says anthropological

Corn varieties from Oaxaca, Mexico. (Courtesy of Pilar Cabrera)

archaeologist David Cheetham. The tortilla was the creation of complex society above a nomadic-band level, one that had the time and resources to take pride in its regional cuisine, dress up the tortilla with elaborate sauces and fillings, and honor their gods and goddesses with the symbol of the cherished tortilla made from the revered corn and prepared with skill and love.

How old is the tortilla? One Aztec legend relates that an anxious peasant hastily grabbed some available corn dough, pressed a misshapen circle, cooked it on a stone slab over the fire, sprinkled it with salt, and handed the first tortilla to a hungry king passing by his hut. But anthropologists focus on the evidence-based ceramic history of the comal, the flat clay griddle with a low side or upturned rim used to cook the dough patted into round tortillas. The specific origin of the tortilla is undetermined, for the presence of the griddle alone might indicate different functions other than making tortillas, remarks anthropologist Barbara Stark. Was an early flat plate used to cook tortillas, or to toast seeds, or to serve food? Was a large griddle with roughened bottom an adaptation to evenly distribute the heat to make the best tortilla? The best griddle to distribute even heat for tortillas was the thin comal. Through daily exposure to the stress of high temperatures over the cooking fire, often the griddle broke. Sorting among the archaeological trash, anthropologists look for an abundance of griddle fragments with corn remains (macrofossil or microfossil) that suggest frequent use of the comal to cook the tortilla staple.

Carbon dating records from comal potsherds do not provide definitive dates and uses, but anthropologists have uncovered potsherds similar to comal remnants in regions and times as diverse as the Valley of Oaxaca around 500–300 BC, and the Basin of Mexico, at Teotihuacán and other sites, around AD 200–650. At Chalcatzingo, about sixty miles south of Mexico City, archaeologist David Grove excavated a 700 BC site layered with processed lime plus pieces of comal-like potsherds. From evidence like this, we are able to guess that the people of the Central Mexico highlands likely prepared nixtamal tortillas around 700 BC. What is certain is the corn tortilla evolved to become an incomparable mainstay of the Mesoamerican cuisine and culture sometime after 300 BC and long before the Hispanic era.

Embracing the Tortilla

The ordinary tortilla was an extraordinary bond between the human and divine. "The tortilla is a perfect circle that breaks away from an undefined mass, like the planets, or by the will of the woman who leaves it to sit on the fire. Prior to this, in the woman's hands or the hands of a god, it was once a sphere, a lump of matter, whose circular shape can be discerned later on, as happens to those who gaze at the sun or at the moon," said Emma Yanes Rizo, an Otomí from Guanajuato, Mexico, in *Tortillas Ceremoniales*.

From birthdays to religious ceremonies, the people of Mesoamerica commemorated important events with tortillas. One

Las Tortilleras, *Carl Nebel lithograph, about 1839. (Courtesy of Nettie Lee Benson Latin American Collection, University of Texas Libraries, University of Texas at Austin)*

Maya tribe even buried their dead with tortillas so that the dogs eaten as dinner during life would not bite the deceased in revenge.

Mesoamericans ate tortillas round or oval and made them from a variety of corn kernels: white, blue, brown, purple, or yellow. Carefully flipped on the comal until "just right" puffy, some were thin, others chubby, large, small, folded around beans for a well-rounded meal, or dipped in chile sauce. The Aztec cut tortillas into wedges and toasted them on a hot griddle to produce *totopochtli*, a prototype of fat-free tortilla chips.

In the Valley of Oaxaca tortillas as lunch-on-the-go coincided with political, cultural, and economic changes between 500–100 BC. At a time of regional population growth, increasing urbanization, and the expansion of hierarchical political institutions, more people farmed greater distances from their homesteads. The corn tortilla folded over wild game or beans (an early type of taco) was a nutritious portable meal for the farmer in the fields at mealtime. "Thus, the increasing importance of the comal and tortilla-making suggests the potential for a more mobile, less purely subsistence labor force that could easily carry meals away from home," says anthropologist Gary Feinman.

Yet in the Maya and the central Gulf lowlands, scant written reference or archaeological evidence of comales to cook the tortilla implies the early Maya for unknown reasons favored tamales—long, thick pieces of corn dough filled with squash or beans, folded inside wet corn husks and boiled or steamed. Around 1000–800 BC the "pots as tools" perspective indicated the lowland Maya prepared nixtamal corn dough. They soaked the corn in large pots of water mixed with the fine caustic powder produced from the local limestone, rinsed it in cast ceramic colanders (pichanchas), and ground it on the metate to create the basic corn dough, masa, suitable for tamales and tortillas. The Maya chose the tamale. The women who wrapped the tamale dough into leaves, steamed and toasted on hot coals, might have saved a bit of the dough and pressed out thick tortillas cooked directly on or under the cooking coals. But the traditional tortilla toasted on the comal was not a widespread choice among the early Maya. When the highlanders from Central Mexico moved into the lowlands it is likely they influenced the Maya with their passion for tortillas. The highlanders knew their tortillas, a tradition inherited from the early civilizations of Teotihuacán and Tula and maintained with flair by the Aztec who created all kinds of recipes for tortillas to satisfy every need and want—even bland tortillas made for fasting without nixtamal corn.

The Spanish Tortilla

Upon their arrival in the New World, the Spanish named the native unleavened flatbread made from corn a "tortilla," a little cake (torta). In 1519, Spanish conquistador Hernán Cortés tasted his first tortilla, a food gift from the Aztec tlatoani, the supreme ruler Motecuhzoma II. Cortés tentatively sampled large, thick quauhtlaquallis or thin, delicate tlacuelpachollis made from tender young white corn, folded around toasted axayacatl (water bugs) or filled with mashed shelled beans, a bit of dried sacrificial blood sprinkled over the top to make the tortillas suitable food for the gods. Cortés was not impressed and preferred his European crusty yeast bread made from wheat to the thin unleavened flat-bread made from corn. When he conquered the Aztec, he vowed to sweep away all remnants of the enemy and bring in new traditions in the name of his Spanish sovereign and the Catholic God. Cortés officially replaced the native Nahuatl word tlaxcalli, "food of gods," with tortilla.

The Spanish replaced more than words. They leveled the Aztec capital Tenochtitlán and on the same footprint built the capital of New Spain, Mexico City. The Europeans substituted the baker for the tortilla maker and installed wood-burning ovens to bake loaves of wheat bread, in their eyes most suitable for the European constitution and the proper nourishment to conquer and colonize. They planted wheat and the native people responded to the new staple by creating the wheat flour version of the tortilla. Even with these challenges, however, the tortilla and its inseparable relationship with the people of Mesoamerica did not entirely fade away with the arrival of Europeans. Today, that indigenous connection with the wheat flour and corn tortilla continues to be strong.

The Corn Tortilla Connection

In the town of Macuilxóchitl in rural Oaxaca, Mexico, the tradition of making "authentic" corn tortillas persists as an important part of the life of the contemporary Zapotec women. The men farm the fields or work at day labor jobs in neighboring towns, while the women produce tortillas for sale in the market and the daily household supply for breakfast and dinner.

Archeologist Ronald Faulseit relates the story of Matilda, who traces back her heritage to the Zapotec culture that flourished in

(left) Pre-Hispanic comal hearth between AD 1000 and 1300, Dainzú-Macuilxóchitl
excavation in Tlacolula, Valley of Oaxaca. (Courtesy of Ronald Faulseit)

(right) Modern comal hearth, Valley of Oaxaca. (Courtesy of Ronald Faulseit)

the Valley of Oaxaca approximately the same time as the ancient
Maya.

> Every morning around 3:30 am, while her husband and chil-
> dren sleep, Matilda wakes up and grinds the corn kernels she
> left soaking in lime water overnight. She gets on her hands
> and knees and rolls the mano over the metate as women have
> for hundreds of years. She heats up her comal hearth with
> reed stems from the river bank. She presses the nixtamal into
> large disks and cooks them to a perfect crispness. She sets a
> few of the tlayudas (large tortillas) aside along with a con-
> tainer of cooked black beans for her husband to take to work.
> Then, she wraps the remaining tlayudas in her rebozo (shawl),
> and walks to the market to sell them for a peso apiece.

When Faulseit excavated a commoner house complex in
Matilda's neighborhood dating about 1000–1200 AD, he found

that the pre-Hispanic Zapotec arranged rectangular sleeping rooms around patios, a cook shed, and the comal hearth. Matilda's home still has this design today. On the patio of one of the excavated homes appeared to be a pre-Hispanic version of the comal hearth of three stones. Matilda's modern hearth looks surprisingly similar.

Even today Matilda sticks to the old ways to prepare the traditional Oaxaca thayuda, a very large, thin, crispy corn tortilla cooked on the large ceramic comal over a hot fire of mesquite or ocote (copel tree) wood, and served covered with refried beans and other toppings. She is proud of her tortillas and prefers the taste and texture of corn ground on the metate and tortillas cooked on a comal instead of baked in factory ovens. With each bit of fresh masa patted into a tortilla round, she affirms her past and nourishes her heritage, and the humble tortilla continues to be an important part of Mesoamerican life.

Chapter 2

• • • THE LIFE-GIVING TORTILLA

Within the walled Sacred Precinct of Templo Mayor in the Aztec city of Tenochtitlán, the children tore a dried-out tortilla in half and, with a piece of the sharp end, played the game of dying on the altar. So went the pretend human sacrifice. Franciscan Fray Bernardino de Sahagún, a Spanish missionary in sixteenth-century New Spain, described the tortilla ritual played by seven children, the chosen ones dedicated to the blue rain god Tlaloc: "Using tortillas of ground corn which had not been softened in lime as mock hearts, they thus cut their hearts out."

But it was no game. In the hands of the Aztec the children gave their own blood to sustain the gods. Five Aztec priests blackened with body paint led the adorned children up the narrow interior stairway and across a landing, up more stairs until they reached the top of the tall pyramidal temple, open to the heavens. Only the priests accessed the immediate area surrounding the sacrificial site, but the people lining the streets and crowding plazas for one of the imperial religious ceremonies of the year knew what happened inside the walls, a reality steeped in their world view of repayment to the gods and in return, renewal of life.

On the flat top of the temple shrine was a ceremonial platform and on the platform a round sacrificial stone altar for the human offering. The priests held each arm and leg. The long, heavy snout of a sawfish known as a carpenter shark kept the head rigid. With a sharp flint knife the high priest swiftly cut the heart out of the still breathing child. He raised the beating heart and offered it to the gods. "These are precious blood-offerings. The rain gods receive them with rejoicing; they wish for them; they are thus satisfied with contentment."

Motivated by hope and fear, the Aztec thanked and placated the rain god for life to the earth. For how could they make the tortillas of feasts and fasts, rituals and daily interactions without rain to grow the corn? If the children cried, and surely most did, the people said the children cried tears of rain.

In myth, the Aztec gods threw themselves into fire to give life to humans. In life, the Aztec paid tribute to the gods with beating hearts for *nextlaulli*, the sacred debt repayment to the gods. Thus, the gods kept the sun revolving and the entire universe in balance for survival in a transitory, often difficult world. Evidence indicated other Mesoamerican groups followed similar practices, although the Spanish exaggerated the massive scale to vindicate the violence unleashed on the "barbarians" of New Spain.

These were people whose gods nurtured yet terrified them. Huitzilopochtli, the mythical war god associated with bloodletting to nourish the sun, named them the Mexica. The Spaniards called them the Aztec. In the beginning the Aztec were hunters and fishers, sometimes settling down to farm and cultivate corn, but seldom remaining long in one place. In 1325 this wandering tribe, known as fearless warriors and one of several Nahuatl-speaking groups called the Chichimeca, migrated from the remote northern deserts to a small swampy island in the middle of Lake Texcoco in the central highlands of Mexico. Less than two hundred years later, hundreds of thousands of people lived in the island city of Tenochtitlán and the towns surrounding the lake. Tenochtitlán (Among the Prickly Pears) was the largest city in the Americas.

The Aztec started with a swamp no one else wanted and transformed it into the promised land of lush gardens, grand canals, and lake produce. Covering over 2,500 acres, the Aztec created a transportation system of canals and causeways, monumental temples, and sprawling open-air markets where merchants traded their wares from as far away as Panama and Nicaragua. They grew foods on raised beds called *chinampas*, small rectangular areas of fertile arable swamp land layered with lake sediment and decaying vegetation, and fenced with poles intertwined with twigs, reeds, and branches. Here on the shallow margins of Lake Texcoco they produced bountiful crops of corn for their prized tortillas. When it rained hard and long all these miraculous accomplishments flooded.

The problem was Tenochtitlán was a salt lake city, a disaster when the nitrous waters overflowed. As the water rose in the landlocked lake it had nowhere to go, no river to the sea. The chinampas that produced bumper crops of corn, beans, squash, and other basic food needs of Tenochtitlán were ruined. Granted, the Aztec supplemented their economy with tributes demanded from its imperial provinces of captives, regional coveted specialties, and mainstay products. Among its tributes, the defeated Tepeacac city-state sent two bins of corn once a year and four thousand loads of processed lime every eighty days to ensure a steady supply of corn tortillas. Yet the Aztec were proud people and they were not going to allow their own environment to defeat them.

Across the lake from Tenochtitlán in Texcoco, Nezahualcóyotl, ally of the Aztec, proposed a solution. When he was not ruling his city-state or writing poetry and philosophizing, Nezahualcóyotl studied architecture and engineering. Under his direction, the citizens of Tenochtitlán completed a levee sealing the fresh waters in the lagoon from the brackish waters of the lake. And they called it the Levee of Poet King Nezahualcóyotl, a system still in place at the time of the Spanish occupation.

Aligned with the Acolhua of Texcoco and the Tepaneca of Tiacopan to form the Aztec Triple Alliance, the Aztec emerged as a daunting military, political, and economic power. At the zenith of the Aztec civilization in the fifteenth and early sixteenth centuries, the war machine gained territory as far south as the border of Guatemala. Merchants traveled far, exchanging turquoise mined in the U.S. Southwest for the sacred plumage of

the scarlet macaws and introduced gold, silver, and copper from
Central and South America. They wrote their history on deer-
skin or bark paper screenfold books preserved with a coat of fine
lime plaster. They competed for civil service positions, studied
astronomy, and lived their days dictated by a fifty-two-year Calendar Round, starting a new cycle as the numbers turned over
every fifty-two years. Into this world came the tortilla.

The Everyday Tortilla

The corn tortilla permeated the Aztec culture, integrated into
almost every aspect of daily life and religion. As nomads the
Aztec likely prepared the simplest tortillas, but once established
in the Valley of Mexico, they assimilated the tradition of the nixtamal tortilla cuisine as a cultural emblem handed down through
generations of the pre-Hispanic peoples of Mexico.

The tortilla provided physical subsistence: "For he who hath no
tortillas, he then fainteth; he falleth down; he droppeth quickly;
there is a twittering as of birds in his ears; darkness descendeth
upon him," wrote Bernardino de Sahagún. It was food fit for
a king and ordinary folk, although the people of Tenochtitlán
lived in a rigid class society, and the tortilla knew its place, fancy
cuisine for the elite or lowly fare for the commoners.

The tortilla was a weapon. On the march to conquer Coyohu-
acán, warriors set up camp and implemented their food strategy, a continuous cooking fire to prepare tortillas folded around
savory lake fowl, fish, and native game. "There, at their gates,
roast, toast, and stew all this (Aztec cuisine), so that the smoke
will enter their city, and the smell will make the women mis-
carry, the children waste away, and the old men and old women
weaken and die of longing and desire to eat that which is unob-
tainable," wrote an anonymous chronicler.

Poets wrote metaphors of the tortilla and artists carved tortillas on ceremonial bowls. Housewives interpreted it as a sign
of an approaching visitor when the tortilla folded on the hot

griddle as if the guest kicked over the tortilla with his stride. At the temple, priests danced with special S-shaped tortillas draped around the neck and offered tortillas in the shape of hands and feet to the gods. On the feast day in the fourth month to honor Centeotl, the maize deity, they dedicated five tortillas in a basket, a dead frog on top that was baked hard, painted blue, and wearing a skirt.

In the palace, the ninth ruler of Tenochtitlán, Motecuhzoma II (Grave Lord) sat on an elaborate cushion before a low table covered with a white woven cloth and decorated with flowers from the cherished palace gardens. He dined on the daily selection of exquisite lime-processed tortillas—thick and large, paper thin and petite, butterfly or leaf shaped, kneaded with eggs, stuffed with duck, turkey, or fish, or sauced in a casserole. As a special item for Motecuhzoma, palace chefs prepared tortillas from red corn kernels ground with a linseed flower and medicinal herbs and roots. Attended by "four very beautiful and clean women," barefoot in front of their ruler, Motecuhzoma ate undisturbed by loud conversation and shielded by a gold screen. At the end of the meal, he drank cacao whipped into foam from a gold cup. "And when he had finished eating, after they ('two other very graceful women') had sung and danced for him, and cleared the table, he took the smoke of one of those pipes, just a little, and with this he fell asleep," recalled Spanish historian Bernal Díaz del Castillo after the conquest of Mexico by the Spaniards in 1521.

In a mud-plastered reed house the farmer sat with his family around the sacred hearth of three stones over a fire pit. In traditional Aztec seated position, men, women, and children kneeled and leaned back on their feet tucked under the body. Using three fingers of the right hand each picked up a plain tortilla, folded it into a cone and scooped up the *molli*, a sauce made of chiles ground with water. On the hot cooking stones sat a pot of corn for tomorrow's tortillas simmered in lime water and today's plain tortillas puffed up on the comal. Next to the hearth was the clay figure of Huehuetéotl, the "Old God" of fire and the hearth. As she cooked, the woman tossed a few pieces of tortilla into the fire, feeding the "Old God." Huehuetéotl was powerful. No Aztec boy wanted to accidently or in anger kick over the hearth stone, for later in battle he would be unable to escape the enemy because his feet would turn numb.

In the open-air market place, thousands of out-of-towners and residents strolled among the stalls and ate tortillas as street food. The tortilla vendor sold squash tortillas, amaranth seed tortillas, tuna cactus tortillas, and tortillas folded over scrambled turkey eggs, combinations of food on the run for the people who could afford it—civil servants, long-distance merchants called *pochteca*, warriors on leave, and the nobility. If quality control slipped and the tortillas tasted bitter or gummy, the vendor attempted to hide the throw-aways, for he did not want to be known as the bad tortilla seller, slovenly and ignorant of the Aztec grand vision of discipline and order. When bits of corn and crumbles of old tortillas fell on the ground, the boys wandering the market picked them up, an Aztec insurance plan in the event a wrathful god watched and brought starvation upon a people who wasted a precious commodity.

A Child's Story

Collecting tortillas scattered on the market floor was not an idle task for a six year old boy. Be useful, his father instructed, and the boy carried firewood into the house and ran errands in the busy marketplace. His sister stayed at home where she practiced spinning while her mother looked over her shoulder, for from the moment the midwife clipped the umbilical cord, boys and girls had separate roles. If the baby was a boy, distinguished warriors buried the umbilical cord in the military practice field. If the baby was a girl, her umbilical cord remained close to home, buried in the hearth under the metate stone for grinding corn. The midwife cut the cord of the baby girl and pronounced, "Thou

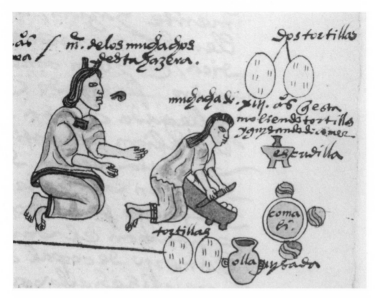

Codex Mendosa. *Aztec mother and child making corn tortillas depicted in the pictorial and textual Aztec account created about 1542 after the Spanish conquest. (Courtesy of Nettie Lee Benson Latin American Collection, University of Texas Libraries, University of Texas at Austin)*

wilt become fatigued, thou wilt become tired; thou art to provide water, to grind maize, to drudge. Thou art to sweat by the ashes, by the hearth."

The typical mother in Tenochtitlán rationed tortillas according to the child's age regardless of the sex. The child turned six years old and ate one and a half tortillas with each meal. The child fell ill, and the healer tied a string around the child's wrists and neck and laid the same allotment of one and a half small green corn tortillas upon the child's chest. From a practical view, a thirteen-year-old ate more than a six-year-old, so food was not wasted. But most important, based on the Aztec belief system of balance and moderation, tortilla rations fulfilled an integral component of becoming an Aztec.

At age nine, the Aztec mother still restricted her child to one and a half tortillas at mealtime, a status quo maintained until thirteen when the tortilla serving increased to two. However, the parents did not withhold a tortilla to punish or offer extra tortillas to reward. When the child did not conform to the Aztec ideal, they were far more inventive with disciplinary techniques than food modification.

When the child was quite young parents reprimanded with a warning or threat, but unusual punishment began at least by nine years old and increased with age. The Codex Mendosa, a pictorial and textual account of early sixteenth-century Aztec life, showed a mother pricking her daughter's wrist with a maguey spike because the child was negligent—perhaps she forgot to flip the tortilla at the precise time on the griddle. The rebellious eleven-year-old boy who ignored his parent's advice fared worse. Bound at his hands and feet, the boy inhaled the irritating chile smoke as his father held him over a fire of burning dry chile. If he cried, it was the Aztec way, for men, women, even the gods cried, a sign of humility.

By age thirteen most children learned well what constituted the ideal Aztec. Anthropologist Frances Berdan describes the hallmark of the exemplary Aztec as "obedience, honesty, discretion, respect, moderation, modesty, and energy." Lofty ideals translated into specific rules of deportment that included the proper way to eat a tortilla. The child washed his hands and sat down to eat. He did not stuff and swallow the whole tortilla in one bite but instead folded the tortilla without breaking it into small pieces. He chewed slowly and ate in moderation. At the end of the meal he picked up any pieces that fell on the ground. Once again he washed his hands and face.

By age fifteen the dutiful daughter perfected the skill of making tortillas. She wanted to be known as a good cook, a requisite for being labeled as a marriageable young woman. In typical dualism of Aztec thought, there was a bad cook and a good cook. The good cook made thick or thin tortillas, round or twisted, honey flavored or folded tortillas filled with chile. She was honest, energetic, and tasted her food before serving. No mother wanted her daughter to be the bad cook—"dishonest, detestable, nauseating, offensive to others . . . sweaty, crude, gluttonous," said Sahagún. The bad cook made smoky, salty, or sour tortillas.

Between the Human and Spiritual World

The Aztec loved their tortillas and believed the tortilla had a soul. "The earth is alive . . . we eat that devotion as corn, we are eating it as tortillas," a present-day Aztec shaman told anthropologist Alan Sandstrom. The shaman lived in a remote village in the lowlands of northern Veracruz, Mexico, once an Aztec Triple Alliance outpost. Linked by history, language, and culture, Nahuatl-speaking curers or ritual specialists (tlamatiquetl) carried on the pre-Hispanic religious rituals of constructing sacred paper images. The shaman, male or female, cut figures specific to spirits out of paper and arranged the images on decorative cut-paper mats called tortilla napkins. "The paper images represent the heart-soul or yolotl of the spirit," says Sandstrom.

Inside the village shrine on the day of Tonantsij, the fertility goddess who ruled over the seed spirits, the shaman knelt before the marigold and palm shrine, the xochicali (flower house), waved copal incense, and chanted over four live chickens. Then he wrung their necks and placed the bodies in front of the altar. The chickens fluttered for a second or two and then died.

The shaman opened his bag of props and pulled out a pair of scissors and paper. In ancient Mesoamerica the shaman used paper made from the bark of the fig tree, or the leaves of the maguey plant, the same desert agave from which the juice is distilled and processed into tequila or mescal. The contemporary shaman used store-bought manufactured paper.

The shaman folded sheets of paper and cut about fifty sets of stacked figures for a curing ritual; sometimes twenty-five thousand figures would be produced for a rain ceremony. Unfolded, the cuttings resembled spirit entities—a person with hands raised by the sides of the head represented the often malevolent wind spirit. An animal-like headdress on a person with arms pointed down represented the earth spirit. On rectangular sheets of paper the shaman constructed tortilla napkins (*tlaxcalli yuyumitl*), intricately cut "beds" to hold the paper spirits. The decorative tortilla napkins compared to the ornamental cloth napkins wrapped around fresh tortillas to keep them warm, moist, and soft. Sorting through hundreds of paper cutouts, the shaman cleansed the spirit entities and prayed for harmony and balance.

But the gods also listened to the Maya. While the warriors of the Triple Alliance rampaged across Mexico from the Pacific Coast to the Atlantic, the Maya people held on to their scattered city-states in southern Mexico, the Yucatán Peninsula, Belize, Guatemala, and parts of Honduras and El Salvador. The splendor of the ancient Maya cities of Petén, Copán, Palenque, and Chichen Itza faded, but the culture did not disappear.

About the time the Aztec basked in the glory of their empire in Central Mexico, the Maya, influenced by trade, mobility, and cookery, promoted the tortilla to an important part of their cuisine. But anthropologist Sophie Coe suggested the Maya women might have been spared the domestic drudgery of the women in highland Mexico who prepared freshly ground corn tortillas three times a day, always served warm off the comal. Spanish Franciscan Fray Diego de Landa and Maya chronicler Gaspar Antonio Xiu described the Yucatán Maya daily meal plan of two meals a day. In the morning the women ground corn for drinks made from nixtamalized corn dough, served for breakfast and lunch. In the evening they ground corn for one solid meal when they ate tortillas and beans flavored with a sauce of ground chiles.

Eventually tortillas rivaled tamales as a mainstay in the Maya daily diet and rituals, a tradition perpetuated by contemporary Maya. The cooks applied the same creativity to the tortilla as they did to the varieties of tamales. In the Yucatán they elevated the

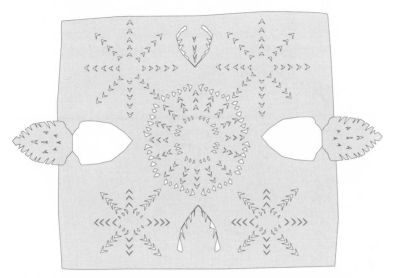

Cut-paper tortilla napkin (bed), used to hold anthropomorphic cut-paper figures of spirit entities during Nahua curing and crop-fertility rituals. Created in 2007 by Nahua curer or ritual specialist María Dolores Hernández, community of Amatlán (a pseudonym), municipio of Ixhuatlán de Madero, Veracruz, Mexico. Illustration by Ana Myers. (Copyright Alan R. Sandstrom and Pamela Effrein Sandstrom, reproduced with permission)

simple enchilada to the classic *papadzules* (food for the nobles)— corn tortillas dipped in a creamy *pepita* (pumpkin seed) sauce, filled with diced hard-boiled bird eggs in place of cheese, yet to be introduced by the Spaniards, and garnished with pureed tomato-chile sauce.

Leonel Pérez, a Mam Maya from Guatemala

Today's Maya have undergone cultural change, but the corn tortilla tradition is deeply ingrained. Leonel Pérez lives in Immokalee, Florida, a town that is home to many of Florida's approximately thirty-three thousand tomato pickers. "I want to tell you a tortilla story," says Pérez. "My grandmother says if you

Leonel Pérez, Mam Maya farm worker from Guatemala in Immokalee, Florida.

have tortillas you have life; if you have corn you have life . . . no need to worry if you have tortillas." Pérez is a Mam Maya who comes from a village in the highlands of Guatemala in the state of Huehuetenango, the last capital on the Pan-American Highway before the Mexican border. In the 1970s and '80s the Maya were caught in the politics and warfare of a civil war between guerrilla and government forces. Guatemala was a country of atrocities and genocide.

Leonel Pérez migrated to Florida when he was twenty-six years old because he saw no other way to lift himself out of poverty. Today he works the farm workers circuit, during the fall and winter picking tomatoes in Florida, and in the summer picking blueberries in North Carolina and New Jersey. Typically, migrant farm labor is one of the lowest paid and most back-breaking jobs in the United States.

In Immokalee, Florida, he connected with a group of farm

laborers, the Coalition of Immokalee Workers, and together with the Florida Tomato Growers Exchange the tomato pickers won an increase in pay. He sends money back home to his parents and grandparents subsisting on two acres of farm land. For generations the Maya people in his village grew corn, their most essential crop to sell as a market crop and the source of tortillas served two or three times a day in the home. They saved seed corn from the previous season, selected for the vigorous ears, and planted four or five seeds per hole "the old way" with the digging stick, the *coa*. A few owned a plow but seldom a tractor. Each farmer watered, weeded, and carefully tended his field during the growing season. "We pay attention to the corn," says Pérez.

The farmers sold their bulk corn in the city market or door-to-door in the village, putting aside enough for their own household. As insurance, if the field yields were low or the market demand high, the women planted rows of corn squeezed among beans and squash in the family kitchen garden. "They were dedicated to making tortillas," says Pérez. His grandmother ground the lime-soaked corn on the metate to make corn dough, the traditional masa, but often his mother walked down the road with her pail of rinsed corn kernels to the local mill and paid the miller to mechanically grind the corn.

Today, Pérez's father grows more coffee than corn in his small field because inexpensive imported corn altered his market. In the supermarket, bags of masa harina, dehydrated corn flour, crowd the shelves, and it is expensive but convenient. Some refuse to buy the processed flour because they believe it interrupted the sacred Maya connection with the land and corn—no comparison between creating tortillas made from nixtamalized corn ground into fresh masa and adding water to premixed corn flour.

Pérez's grandfather thinks the masa harina produces an inferior tortilla. "I can't stand the smell," he says. But every now and then Pérez's mother uses the corn flour mix, freeing her to work in the house garden where she grows produce to sell in the local Thursday market.

In Immokalee, Pérez buys his daily supply of corn tortillas from the local tortillería. The tortillas retain a bit of the lime flavor from the factory processed nixtamal corn flour and are fresh, no preservatives, loosely wrapped in paper while still warm. "Of course, I miss my mother's tortillas, but I got used to the taste," he says.

Nakara

"Don't we all eat from the same tortilla?" said a Nuyooteco elder who lives today in the indigenous Mixtec community of Santiago Nuyoo in the mountainous southwestern region of Oaxaca, Mexico. Whether made from scratch or packaged flour, the corn tortilla as a source of food, meaning, and emotions connects the Mesoamerican descendants of the corn people from the sandy flatlands of Immokalee, Florida, to the high end of the canyon in Nuyoo, Oaxaca.

On a typical cool mountain morning, a Nuyooteco family gathered on the patio in the detached kitchen shed to warm themselves before the cooking fire and share the morning meal. Ensuring a steady supply of warm tortillas, the mother, up since 3 or 4 a.m. to prepare the dough, stood and cooked the tortillas, only pausing long enough to taste a bit of her husband's tortilla. The father filled his tortilla from a selection of beans, eggs, meat flavored with cilantro, and a variety of chile sauces. He broke off pieces of his breakfast tortilla for the children. To drink, the mother might have saved some of the masa, the dough used to make tortillas, and thickened a warm and hearty pre-Hispanic drink, champurrado, a chocolate-based atole. The family drank from the same cup, scooped food out of the same bowl, and ate from the same tortilla.

The Nuyootecos had nakara for each other, "a willingness to

take responsibility for another by providing what is needed
for a healthy life," says anthropologist John Monaghan. Nakara
expressed a strong collective bond between parents and their
children, the "great house" of the community, and the Mixtec
culture. But when asked, Nuyootecos defined nakara as the giving of food and clothing, the most intimate way they gave form
to their relationships. The Mixtec wedding celebrated both.

"Just as the tortilla is a 'blessing' from god, so too a woman
is a 'blessing' from another household," said the Nuyootecos. In
marriage, the Nuyootecos transferred household responsibilities
and created a new domestic unit, symbolized by the staple tortilla. "I believe that from your house will come the tortillas I
will eat and the water I will drink," said the intended husband
to his future in-laws. In marriage, the Nuyootecos expected "an
infusion of life," for continuity depended on a new generation
of children.

On the wedding day, typically the couple were married in the
morning in a civil service performed by a municipal official,
often saving a church service blessed by the priest for a month
or two later. In the evening, they were married at the Mixtec
wedding, viko tana'a, celebrated at the groom's household with
plenty of beer, meat dishes, and tortillas. For the Mixtec ceremony, the bride wore wedding clothes provided by the groom's
godparents while the bride's godparents clothed the groom, an
exchange of roles that solidified the ties between the two different families.

At the wedding table the bride and groom sat before a large
plate of tortillas prepared from corn varieties grown from the
families' heirloom seeds. "Eat and grow together," said the
groom's godfather, and he tore the top tortilla in half and formed
the two halves into a tortilla cross. The bride ate the top half
while the groom ate the bottom, eating to speak as one, sustain
each other, and grow old as one heart, one mind.

The tortilla was more than nourishment and culinary pride.

The tortilla was their "flesh and blood," rooted in the sacred corn. Folded, the tortilla was a metaphor for the female sexual organs. It was a form of "gifting," an opportunity to exchange gifts of tortillas. And, more than a token ritual, the Nuyootecos said by eating the tortilla together the couple completed themselves.

And so the tortilla implies a distinct definition of life giving. But how was the tortilla able to survive when pitted against European bread when the Spanish arrived in Mesoamerica?

Chapter 3

• • • THE STUBBORN TORTILLA

The tortilla journeyed through Mesoamerica as the star and then the bit player of New Spain. On April 22, 1519, eleven Spanish brigantines carrying over five hundred soldiers, horses, dogs, a crew of sailors, European matchlock guns, and fourteen cannons sailed into the port of Veracruz, Mexico. Spanish conquistador Hernán Cortés began his conquest of Mexico. Cortés wanted gold, silver, and a colony for the glory of his sovereign ruler Charles V, the Roman Catholic Church, and himself. Motecuhzoma II, the ninth tlatoani who ruled the Aztec empire, wanted the Spaniards to simply go away.

Perhaps Cortés, a formidable mortal threat or the god Quetzalcóatl incarnate, could be appeased, persuaded to abandon his plan to trek almost two hundred miles across the hot, humid coastal plains through mountain passes to the highlands of the Valley of Mexico and confront Motecuhzoma. Motecuhzoma ordered the high priest Teoctlamacazqui the tlillancalqui (Keeper of the House of Darkness) to the coast.

At the harbor, Teoctlamacazqui met Cortés and presented lavish gifts of gold, turquoise and jade jewelry, quetzal plume headdresses threaded with gold, jaguar skins, and woven clothing. He offered Aztec war captives and told Cortés he could use them for slaves or a blood sacrifice. He offered fine, white corn tortilla dishes reserved for Aztec lords, lush fruits, and the prized cacao drink. "The ambassador then ordered that the food be placed in front of the newcomers and their horses, and in their ingenuous manner they gave one turkey to each soldier and another to his horse, a basket of tortillas for the master and another for the animal. This was done until they were told that the beasts ate only corn and grass and soon the Aztec envoys provided the animals with the latter," wrote Dominican missionary Fray Diego Durán.

Cortés was polite but ignored Motecuhzoma. Guided by the Totonacs, enemies of the Aztec, Cortés and his army marched into the thick of Aztec territory toward the capital of Tenochtitlán. "They were very white, their eyes were like chalk. Their armaments, their swords, their shields, their lances, were all of iron. The animals they rode were as high as a roof top and looked like deer. Their dogs were huge, their eyes blazed, yellow like fire. They moved about with their tongues hanging, always panting," said an Aztec elder years after the conquest.

Along the route, the awed villagers gave the Spaniards food and drink. The women handed the intruders hot tortillas seasoned with honey or chile or folded around beans. In the late afternoon Cortés made camp and engaged "Indian women who were good for grinding maize for bread. . . . they were given little beads." For now, the Spaniards ate the diet of the Aztec, corn tortillas. Tortillas were substance food on the road, rations in battle, communion wafers at church, and delicacies at feasts. No wheat fields, no mills, no millers, no bakers, no bread.

On November 8, 1519, Cortés crossed the main causeway leading to the Aztec capital of Tenochtitlán in the middle of Lake Texcoco. Inside the fortified city gates Motecuhzoma met Cortés. "After we had crossed this bridge, Mutezuma came to greet us and with him some two hundred lords, all barefoot and dressed in a different costume, but also very rich in their way and more so than the others. They came in two columns, pressed very close to the walls of the street, which is very wide and beautiful and so straight that you can see from one end to the other," said Cortés.

"Tell Motecuhzoma that we are his friends and that there is nothing to fear. We have waited long to meet with him," said

Cortés. Within a week Cortés imprisoned Motecuhzoma in his own palace where the last independent ruler of the Aztec empire died, either wounded by a sling stone thrown by his disillusioned people during a skirmish with the Spanish or assassinated by one of Cortés's followers. Those who told the story of Motecuhzoma's death—the Spaniards writing their history or native recollections recorded by the Spaniards—did not know for certain the cause or did not admit the truth. Within nine months Cortés declared victory in the name of Charles V, although subsequent rulers Cuitláhuac and Cuauhtemoc fought the Spaniards until the final surrender on August 13, 1521.

Defeated by guns and cannons, steel armor, horses, political and military tactics, fierce Tlaxcalan warriors enlisted by Cortés, famine, and smallpox, the great Aztec civilization fell. "And so the war ended, we laid down our shields. We have suffered enough! Some fled across the lake, others across the causeways. Spanish soldiers stopped people everywhere, looking for gold. They stripped the women, even peering into their mouths. As for the men, many were taken and branded on the cheeks," said a conquered Aztec.

Stone by stone, plot by plot, the Spaniards dismantled the heart of the Aztec world, Tenochtitlán, and on top of the ruins built the capital of New Spain, Mexico City. Within three years Spanish bakers baked wheat bread in brick ovens and swine roamed the streets. In the marketplace, separate from the indigenous market, farmers sold fruit and vegetables, lake fowl and game, familiar food for the European palate—the proud tortilla vendors were gone. In the cathedral, once the site of an Aztec temple, Spanish ladies covered their head and shoulders with a black lace mantilla to pray to their Catholic God. Administered by the Spanish viceroy accountable to Charles V through the Council of the Indies, Mexico City became home for an increasing influx of Spanish colonists. For the diminished Aztec population, most of whom died or fled, their prized city was no longer home, forced by the foreigners to adapt to new food, religion, politics, and economics wrapped around an alien language.

A New Spain Banquet

Food was a large part of the pride and endeavor of the New Spain settlers in Mexico. Earlier in 1494, Christopher Columbus theorized that conflict and disease struck the colonists in the Spanish Caribbean colony of Hispaniola because the European constitution did not thrive in the new climate. He said, eat what you ate in Spain. The colonists living in the unfamiliar environment of Mexico remembered his words. Although they embraced the bounty of New World fruits and vegetables, they were anxious about their diet. European food—especially wheat bread, beef and pork, olive oil, and red wine—was substance for their survival and identity. No wonder they were suspicious of the tortilla, equally as significant to the natives as bread was to the Spanish.

In 1538 the viceroy of Mexico City, Antonio de Mendoza, and the Marqués del Valle, aka Hernán Cortés, shared celebratory toasts of mead, the honey wine made from New World bees, and wine, Spanish imports made from old world grapes. They raised gold leaf goblets confiscated from Aztec lords. To Charles V, Emperor of Spain! To Frances I, King of France! For across the Atlantic Ocean Spain and France signed a tenuous peace treaty and the loyal Spanish subjects in Mexico City demonstrated they cared by holding a party.

In the plaza, the guests sat at tables staged around fountains of cascading water, parrots flying between fruit trees, and one odd jaguar on a short chain. Servants paraded among the guests with an enormous amount of food, too much to consume but intended to impress. In the center of each table, the servers placed platters of stuffed ducks and geese with silvered beaks and feet, and mysterious oversized pies. Simultaneously the servers opened all the pies and out popped live rabbits and birds. How they contained the creatures until the appointed moment was not explained.

Mole Poblano

The seventeenth-century Sisters of the Santa Rosa Convent in Puebla, Mexico, are credited with creating *mole poblano*, a popular Mexican regional dish that rivals the American taco. One legend claims the angels gave the Sisters the recipe; another claims it was borrowed from the Aztec. Mole poblano is a blend of indigenous and European foods, cuisine developed after the Spanish conquest. This recipe is courtesy of Pati Jinich, cookbook author and chef at the Mexican Cultural Institute in Washington, D.C. (http://www.patismexicantable.com). Jinich uses corn tortillas to thicken and flavor the recipe, and she serves the dish with corn tortillas.

Mole Poblano: Adapted from Sor Andrea
de la Asunción from the Santa Rosa Convent
Serves 24–25

Ingredients:
½ cup lard, vegetable shortening or vegetable oil
(Reserve the seeds from all chiles)
3 oz chiles anchos, about 6 or 7, stemmed and seeded
3 oz chiles pasillas, about 12 or 13, stemmed and seeded
3 oz chiles mulatos, about 6, stemmed and seeded
⅓ oz dried chipotle chiles, about 4, stemmed and seeded
½ white onion, about ½ pound, roughly chopped
3 garlic cloves, peeled and roughly chopped
3 tablespoons raw almonds with skin
3 tablespoons raw shelled peanuts
3 tablespoons raisins
1 tablespoon pumpkin seeds
4 tablespoons sesame seeds
½ cup reserved chile seeds
5 whole cloves, stemmed
¼ teaspoon anise seeds
¼ teaspoon coriander seeds
½ teaspoon whole black peppercorns
1 stick true or ceylon cinnamon
¼ teaspoon ground allspice
⅛ teaspoon dried thyme
⅛ teaspoon dried marjoram

(continued on next page)

½ lb roma tomatoes, about 2, charred or roasted
⅓ lb tomatillos, about 2, husked, rinsed, charred/roasted
2 corn tortillas, sliced in 8 pieces
½ bolillo, telera or baguette, about 2 oz, thickly sliced (if it is
    a couple days old, better)
6 oz Mexican style chocolate or bittersweet chocolate
5 cups chicken broth (plus 4 more cups to dilute later on)
1 teaspoon kosher or sea salt, or more to taste
½ cup sesame seeds, toasted, to sprinkle at the end

To Prepare:
In a large extended casserole dish set over medium high heat, add
½ cup lard, oil, or vegetable shortening. Once hot, about 2 minutes
later, add the chiles in 2 or 3 batches and sauté, stirring often, and
being careful not to let them completely burn. Remove with a slot-
ted spoon and place in a mixing bowl as you move along.

In the same oil, add chopped onion and garlic and sauté for 2 to
3 minutes, stirring, until they soften and release their aroma. Stir
in the almonds, peanuts, raisins and pumpkin seeds, and let them
cook for 2 to 3 minutes.

Stir in the sesame seeds, reserved chile seeds, stemmed cloves,
anise seeds, coriander seeds, black peppercorns, cinnamon stick,
ground allspice, thyme and marjoram. Stir frequently and let it all
cook for 3 to 4 more minutes, stirring often. Make room again,
and add the tortilla and bread pieces along with the tomatoes and
tomatillos. Let it all cook for a couple minutes.

Incorporate the already sautéed chiles and pour in the chicken
broth. Stir and once it comes to a simmer, add the chocolate
pieces and the salt. Mix well, and let it simmer for 12 to 15 minutes. Turn off the heat, cover and let the mix rest for ½ hour, so
the chiles can completely soften.

In batches, puree the mixture in the blender or food processor
until smooth. You can store this mole, covered, in the refrigerator
for up to a month, or freeze it for up to a year.

When ready to eat, dilute a cup of mole with ½ cup chicken
broth in a saucepan and simmer for 2 to 3 minutes. Serve over
cooked chicken or turkey and sprinkle with toasted sesame seeds
on top.

The diners ate whole suckling pig and roasted goat, pork, and beef, boiled mutton, quail pies, chicken casseroles, and crusted empanadas made from bread dough formed into small pies filled with fish or game. They ate white wheat bread served with cheese and olives. For dessert, sweet marzipan and fruit tortes were presented to the guests. To drink, the delicious foamy chocolate drink cacao was poured for the assembled, an Aztec concession on the European menu.

In the banquet kitchen, the Spanish cooks seasoned their familiar foods with native herbs and imported spices. They used lard from European-bred hogs as cooking fat and Mediterranean olive oil and vinegar as marinade. Mesoamerican pungent chiles were for "throats lined with tin," corn was fed to livestock, and tortillas were as segregated as the two distinct societies of Españoles and Indios. Yet the tortilla makers, the Aztec women of Tenochtitlán who ground the corn and patted the dough, were there on this night of European pride. They were in the kitchen, put to work by the boss cooks, rolling out pie crusts and punching down yeast dough to shape into rolls.

The Wheat People

Change began with economics. The Mother Country of Spain was ambitious but poor, grappling with messy European politics, religious alliances, military adversaries, and agricultural disasters. Send back riches to Spain, but you are on your own, Mexico.

Soon after Charles V declared the territory of Mexico a colony, dockhands loaded cattle, goats, sheep, swine, and horses on ships transporting successive waves of colonists from Spain's southern ports across the Atlantic Ocean. In the new colony, it seemed to the newcomers that the New World was overwhelmingly abundant. They savored the sweet tropical fruits. The adventurers in search of gold and silver headed for the mining towns emerging in the hill country. Drafted native laborers cut trees from virgin forests for Mexico City's buildings and fuel. The hacienda owner introduced a new style of agriculture, ranching. Cattle grazed on usurped cornfields or fallow land abandoned by the displaced indigenous Mexicans. The first group of farmers selected the best cropland with a water source, hooked draft animals to the iron plow, and turned over the fertile river bottom soil to plant market wheat, a source of income.

Wheat produced less grain than corn per acre and demanded more attention and investment than the cultivation of corn, yet the Spanish hacienda owners planted a large part of estate land in wheat to meet the demand for bread. Other commercial farmers planted corn introduced by the Mesoamericans to the Europeans and accepted as a worthy and adaptable grain, but corn made tortillas—Indio food associated with going native. Wheat turned into bread, a sign of Old World civilization in a wild New World. Without bread, the colonists would lose part of their culture.

When Motecuhzoma bit into a small piece of heavy wheat bread he said it tasted "like chaff, like dried maize stalks." The Spanish said the fluffy corn tortillas made without lard or oil tasted insipid. The Spanish good baker replaced the Aztec good tortilla maker and the colonists trusted only an experienced European miller to grind wheat into smooth, fine flour. At the gristmill, the miller—a bit perplexed by the native tortilla makers who ground corn, bent over the metate—imported Old World technology to grind grains into pounds of flour using a water-powered wheel. But the women who made the tortillas and the men who ate them insisted that mill-ground cornmeal was not the same as the traditional lime-infused masa molded into a tasty flatbread. Thus, the Europeans ate bread, and the native Mexicans ate tortillas . . . unless they were served bread as work rations, the corn crop failed, or they wanted to disso-ciate themselves from their disenfranchised and impoverished neighbors.

Typically the conquered owed the conquerors. The colonists latched onto a short term solution to self-sufficiency. Under the encomienda system the Spanish assigned disenfranchised and fragmented indigenous communities to individual conquistadors who demanded payments of labor and tributes in return for physical care and spiritual salvation. Loyal to the new authority, demoted former Aztec elite and newly appointed local chiefs—the privileged class of caciques—recruited laborers and collected tributes.

In Mexico City, the Cortés compound depended on its weekly tribute to supplement the kitchen garden and barnyard supply of eggs and meat. Each week an Indio pulled his cart to the servant's entrance to deliver fifteen loads of corn, bulk salt, and bundles of firewood. Throughout the week he supplied fresh native fowl, chickens, rabbits, quail, and a steady provision of seasonal fruit. But who ate the tortillas listed in the Cortés household account totaling eighty baskets a week, each filled with twenty tortillas? Cortés and his fashionable guests only ate tortillas out of necessity, but the native servants, too busy attending to Cortés and friends to make their own tortillas, were used to fresh tortillas three times a day.

The colonists' source of labor and tributes backfired. In the first sixty years of the occupation an estimated 90 percent of the indigenous population died from disease. Dissipated by illness, exploitation, and poverty, those remaining could not keep up with the colony's needs. Most significant, the system interrupted the communal sacred relationship with earth, sun, water, and corn. After toiling a long day in the fields or mines or household estates, the corn people were tired. Some were too worn out to farm their small milpa, the home plot where subsistence corn, beans, and squash grew together, and the land reverted to its wild state. But many refused to break the tie with their land and history. The farmer stuck the digging stick, the coa, into the soil, said a prayer, and sowed hills of corn planted in rows. He hoed weeds and harvested the crop, stored until ready to be ground into corn dough for tortillas. Without tortillas, the Mexicans would lose part of their culture.

In 1549 repartimiento replaced encomienda. Under the repartimiento system, intended to abolish indigenous slavery, the Spanish assigned the natives rotating compulsory jobs for low wages. Occasionally the natives negotiated the complex colonist relationship and successfully protected their personal land and labor. Often employers withheld pay or overworked the natives.

Tortilla Conversions

But while the Spaniards attended to the basic needs of food, clothing, and shelter they did not forget their spiritual mission, to save souls. Swiftly the conquistadors eliminated the elite rulers and priestly leadership concentrated in the Aztec metropolises and destroyed the special ceremonial centers where warriors, nobles, and priests performed rituals dedicated to their gods and goddesses. Then the conquerors passed the job of conversion to the Christian God to the friars and priests. And some particularly zealous friars improvised with tortilla conversions.

Tortilla. This was a catchword in the campaign to further the conversion of the indigenous people of Mexico to Catholicism. "First of all it is necessary that you believe the most Holy Sacrament is made with wine and with tortillas," recorded Domingo de San Antón Muñon Chimalpahin Quauhtlehuanitzin in *Exercicio quotidiano*, the sixteenth-century religious manuscript attributed to Fray Bernardino de Sahagún. In tiny chapels throughout the conquered regions spreading out from Mexico City, the friars gathered the villagers and taught daily devotional meditations and spiritual introspection. "Here, written in the Mexican language (Nahuatl) begins a manual of spiritual prudence taken from the Holy Gospel divided into each of the days with which a week is completed."

On Sunday, the indigenous people adapting to a changing

colonial world contemplated the Last Supper. "And when our Lord Jesus Christ had thus spoken, then He took tortillas and gave them to the apostles. He said, This that I give you is My Body, which because of you is to be betrayed into others' hands," the friar preached. "And when the priest has uttered the word of God that is called consecration over the tortillas and the wine, then the tortillas are changed into the precious body of our Lord Jesus Christ and the wine is changed into His precious blood. They are no longer in any way tortillas; nor is that wine there."

The adapted sacrament described in *Exercicio quotidiano* tested papal authority, for the Roman Catholic Church insisted on wheat for the Holy Eucharist bread. Did the friars manipulate the symbolic meaning of corn, sacred to the villagers, to facilitate mass baptism? Or were they pragmatic, the bread sent by the city bakers moldy and inedible by the time it reached the provinces, and substituted with a piece of tortilla dissolved in the mouth at the communion altar? As a spiritual precaution, the friars persuaded each tortilla maker to make the sign of the cross when she patted the dough and cooked the tortilla on the griddle.

Officially, the Roman Catholic Church converted the perceived pagans into Christians. The priests of one God replaced the priests of the gods, calendar day saints festivals replaced tribal rituals, and places of worship changed from urban temples and rural mountaintop shrines to Catholic chapels and cathedrals. Yet in private lives and attitudes the traditional rituals and beliefs of the indigenous people reshaped elements of Christian observance.

The Ceremonial Tortilla

By the mid-sixteenth century the Spanish were on the move. It was 1550 and the Spanish colonists invaded the Otomí farming communities along the Laja River in Guanajuato, Mexico. Known for their negotiating skills, for a time the Otomí preserved their

Ceremonial tortilla
with an image of a
rooster painted by the
Otomí in Querétaro,
Mexico. (Courtesy of
Teresa Galindo and
Karina Jazmín Juárez
Ramírez, Tortillas
Ceremoniales,
Centro de las Artes del
Guanajuato, Mexico)

strong local government and rights to the precious corn land in exchange for converting to Catholicism and paying tributes. A peaceful way to deal with the enemy, the Otomí must have thought, until the Spanish warred with the neighboring Chichimeca and enlisted the Otomí to help with a war that went on and on until 1600. Inevitably Spanish ways dominated the Otomí culture, but over the centuries the Otomí retained their identity and traditions by fusing Catholic beliefs with pre-Hispanic rituals.

The Otomí belonging to "The Region of the River" respected and worshiped their environment, even talked to the earth, plants, rivers, sun, clouds, and rocks. They based most of their rituals around farming, especially corn. The corn tortilla as the ritual food offering was a natural and meaningful expression of their world. Before the Spanish arrived the Otomí painted ceremonial tortillas with images associated with the earth and their gods. After the Spanish occupation the Otomí mixed the old with the new. They included Catholic patron saints in their tortilla motifs.

Today, ceremonial tortilla painting is still specific to the Otomí communities of this region and certain neighboring communities in Querétaro. Otomí-painted tortillas are shaded yellow from local corn and imprinted with colorful festive images linked to religious ceremonies, community events, or private family celebrations. For special occasions ceremonial painted tortillas were both offering and food. On the feast day to honor each town's patron saint, members of the community placed ceremonial tortillas upon the chapel altar as ritual offerings of veneration and praise. The women who made batches of tortillas stood outside the chapel and shared tortillas, wrapped in napkins to keep warm, as food for visitors and the participants in the festival.

The night before the ceremonial day, the women prepared two of their favorite colors of plant dye commonly used by the Aztec. For purple, they boiled honeysuckle flowers and soaked the flowers in the water until the liquid thickened. For shades of maroon from red to brown, they scraped off the white scale on the flat pads of the nopal plant and slid the scale into pots of boiling water until the heat released its color. Nopal, a regional species of *Opuntia*, prickly pear cactus, is a host plant for the cochineal scale insect. When the female cochineal inserts the proboscis, the tube, into the pad for food, she secretes a white scale for camouflage and a shield against dryness. An astringent maroon pigmentation repels ants and other predators and produces the dye.

Typically the men made the tortilla molds, the *pintaderas*, flat square or round blocks of mesquite hardwood carved to imprint images on tortillas. A daughter inherited the mold from her mother or a mother-in-law passed the mold to her daughter-in-law. The craftsman penciled the design on the wood and chiseled with a knife an image, his choice or a personal request. For Holy Week he might be commissioned to carve a representation

Ceremonial painted tortillas cooking on the comal at an Otomí festival in Querétaro, Mexico. (Courtesy of Teresa Galindo and Karina Jazmín Juárez Ramírez, Tortillas Ceremoniales, Centro de las Artes del Guanajuato, Mexico)

of the Otomí Holy Cross with earth images of corn or chiles combined with Jacob's Ladder or the rooster, icons that symbolized the Passion. At the beginning of the farming season or at harvest time, he carved San Ysidro, the Catholic patron saint of farmers. And he produced molds of cultural significance to the Otomí: a woman grinding corn, a cornfield, an eagle, or a flower.

On the morning of the ceremonial day, in the open-air kitchen, grandmother and mother and daughter dipped a corn cob into a solution of pigment extracted from the cochineal insect and rolled the cob like a rolling pin over a carved mesquite mold to coat the high relief image with color. The pigment stained their hands several shades of deep maroon.

It was hot on the patio where the women worked. Kettles of pigment steamed on the outdoor stove and griddles heated over the open wood fire. The women took turns working together. The granddaughter coated the mold with color until the pigment dried while her grandmother partially cooked the tortilla. Timed precisely, her grandmother took the tortilla off the griddle and carefully placed it on the mold. With the palm of her hand she spread the tortilla over the mold and the color seeped from the image into the soft, warm dough. Only a few seconds and she removed the tortilla from the mold. Her granddaughter made the sign of the cross over the griddle and finished cooking the tortilla, painted side down, the image sealed onto the tortilla. Once the women cooked all the tortillas, they prepared the meal, served with "the cross of the griddle," two joined circles made from corn dough. They created an art and continued a legacy that can be traced back to the Spanish conquest.

The Travel Tortilla

From Central Mexico the Spanish conquistadors moved south and east into Puebla and Oaxaca and tackled the Maya territory. In 1523, the ruthless Pedro de Alvarado, oblivious to the civility of a world unlike his own, swept through the highlands of Chiapas, Mexico, and Guatemala. He did not make the hard ocean crossing from Spain to make friends; he wanted riches. Alvarado dismissed the Maya as feebleminded people "who only ate tortillas dipped in water mixed with ground chile."

In 1549 Franciscan Fray Diego de Landa was one of the zealous Spanish missionaries eager to conquer the Maya with conversions in the Yucatán Peninsula, Mexico. While he crusaded for Spain and Christianity, Landa lived among the Maya, learned their language, and ate Maya "bread"—tortillas and tamales. He and his fellow missionaries struggled to convert the Maya who adhered to their spiritual beliefs and rituals and refused to confess their "sins." Frustrated and angry, Landa resorted to torture and murder, and he burned shrines, religious icons, and the printed books filled with the history of the Yucatán Maya

Viceroyalty of New Spain map around 1650. (Tom Wilbur; redrawn from the map of Viceroyalty of New Spain, The Colonial Heritage of Latin America, University of Dayton, Ohio)

civilization. In time, he killed more than he converted, and his Bishop in Spain ordered Landa to return home for trial. With time on his hands as his religious superiors deliberated, and no one to convert, Landa wrote *Relación de las Cosas de Yucatán*, a detailed account of Maya customs and languages. He was absolved of wrongdoing and eventually reassigned to the Yucatán and ordained bishop.

But in the lowland Yucatán Peninsula, groups of the stubborn Lacandón Maya fled the Spanish. They abandoned their villages and retreated deeper and deeper into the jungle forests, fortified by their reliable corn dough drink called *keyem* by the Maya, but commonly known as posolli, and travel tortillas. At home the women made fresh soft and puffy tortillas, warm off the comal. For the road, they made the travel tortilla, a sourdough tortilla, from corn dough stored overnight with a small amount of mother culture from previous soured dough. The women toasted the tortillas until crisp, portable survival food. Today about 250 to 500 unconquered Lacandón still invoke their ancestral gods at crumbling temples, struggling to survive land loss, lumbered jungles, mass tourism, and politics.

Undaunted by harsh terrain and rebellious natives, the Spanish expanded their territory as far north as Durango and Sonora and then focused their ambitions on the northern border of Mexico and what is now the Southwest United States. Along the route, first the priests baptized the natives they encountered, then the colonists established towns, raised cattle, and introduced wheat. And the corn tortilla slid down the list as the flour tortilla was born and came up in the world.

Chapter 4

• • • EL NORTE

In July 1542, it was hot and dusty in the Pueblo country of northern New Mexico. By the time the Spanish exploratory expedition reached Háwikuh, the southernmost of the Zuni pueblos, conquistador Francisco Vásquez de Coronado, dressed to conquer in a gilded suit of full armor and metal helmet adorned with plumes, was exhausted and hungry. He was happy for the substance of "Indian tortillas."

Coronado and his army of Spanish soldiers and an intimidating force of indigenous reinforcements from Mexico sometimes marched in military formation but often trudged in broken rank. The travelers moved over rugged mountains and through bleak deserts from Central Mexico to the northern frontier of New Spain into Arizona, Pima tribal territory, and farther north into New Mexico. They searched for the legendary golden Seven Cities of Cibola.

For all who listened to his speculations, Franciscan priest and explorer Marcos de Niza painted a vivid picture of a rumored native kingdom called Cibola equal to the riches and power of Motecuhzoma's Aztec empire. Coronado and his soldiers grumbled. Instead of a sparkling metropolis with ceremonial temples reaching toward the sky and streets paved of gold, Coronado found six isolated Zuni pueblo villages the color of various shades of brown. Boxy communal multi-storied homes layered with an adobe pudding mix of mud blended with straw and water surrounded a brushed dirt ceremonial plaza. The only gold was Zuni gold: acres of fields planted with corn.

"It now remains for me to tell about the Seven Cities, the kingdom and province, of which the father provincial gave your Lordship an account. Not to be too verbose, I can assure you that he has not told the truth in a single thing that he said, but everything is the opposite of what he related, except the name of the cities and the large stone houses," said Coronado.

Coronado demanded submission and food. "The food which they eat in this country consists of maize, of which they have great abundance, beans and game . . . They make the best tortillas that I have ever seen anywhere, and this is what everybody ordinarily eats. They have the very best arrangement and method for grinding that was ever seen. One of these Indian women here will grind as much as four of the Mexicans do," said Coronado.

Fortunately for Coronado, the proud Mexican woman who spent over six hours a day soaking and rinsing lime-treated corn, grinding the kernels into smooth dough, and patting into perfectly round tortillas did not hear his sentiment. But the tired Coronado was impressed with the Zuni corn-grinding assembly line and the variety of tasty cornbreads the women produced to feed the famished foreigners who rode into their world. Possibly Coronado labeled any form of corn patties as tortillas because they were round and made from ground corn, but the Southwest Pueblo did not prepare the traditional Mesoamerican nixtamal tortilla.

Coronado watched groups of three or four women kneel at multiple metates, the grinding stones set at an angle to the ground and fitted into individual stone troughs to create a metate house. The women waited until an elder, retired from corn grinding, spread her blanket, sat cross-legged, and began to chant a corn song about earth and sky and fire and water. Synchronized to the beat of the music, the woman at the beginning of the line took the flat stone mano in both hands and crushed the toasted dried corn kernels on the rough grinding stone. From various degrees of coarse to fine grinding stones, the women passed the corn down the line until ground into different grades of cornmeal. At the end of the morning, the women divided the ground corn into equal shares to take home.

Maybe a woman used her share to make dumplings or Zuni traveling bread or tortilla-like corn cakes. Maybe she dried yellow or white corn and treated it with a solution of wood or plant ashes to make hominy, the corn dough basis for tamales or tortillas. Or maybe she offered a prayer to the kachina (the ancestor spirit) of the Blue Corn Woman and kneaded blue cornmeal dough prepared from the ground kernels of the revered blue corn plant, shaped into blue cornbread patties or boiled blue marbles or blue cornmeal mush wrapped in corn husks.

Like the young Aztec woman of marriageable age who mastered the art of making tortillas, the suitable Zuni bride tutored by her mother and grandmother learned to prepare perfect paperbread, called *hewe* by the Zuni, *piki* by the Hopi, and *mowa* by the Rio Grande Tewa. Unlike the Mesoamerican nixtamal preparation, she ground the blue corn into meal before she added the wood ash or lime solution. The batter inherited the additional nixtamal nutrients and the lime preserved the dark blue color of the cooked paperbread. Sweeping a thin handful of batter over a hot flat stone supported on four stones at each corner, she baked transparent rectangular sheets of the blue-grey wafer bread, served rolled up like a newspaper.

Soon Coronado, well fed and rested, proclaimed the Zuni conquered and, looking for the elusive gold, pushed onward to present-day Kansas before he returned home to Mexico City, empty-handed and in debt.

Nuevo Mexico

More than fifty years later the Spaniards returned to colonize the first European settlement in New Mexico. In March 1598, Juan de Oñate (distinguished in marriage to Isabel de Tolosa Cortés

Motecuhzoma, a descendant of conquistador Hernán Cortés and Aztec emperor Motecuhzoma) led a colonizing expedition of a culturally and racially mixed troop of about five hundred full-blooded Spaniards, criollos (Mexican-born Spaniards), mestizos (mixed Spanish and indigenous ancestry), mulattos (part European and African), and indigenous Mexican servants. Recent historical research also indicates that the colonists likely included a small discreet contingent of Sephardic Jews, originally from Iberia. They were the crypto-Jews, or "hidden Jews," who fled from Spain to Mexico City and then to northern Mexico and New Mexico to escape the Inquisition.

The colonists were traders, farmers, ranchers, artisans, Franciscan priests and nuns, soldiers, and miners. Oñate enticed their participation with a promise of land for the less than noble. For those who were not descended from royal blood but were of good standing with money, he conferred the title hidalgo, the lowest order of nobility. Once privileged as a hidalgo the colonist was exempt from paying taxes and able to purchase land through Spanish land grants.

They traveled with seven thousand heads of livestock, pieces of artillery, covered wagons, and ox carts. Oñate rode horseback until he tired and retreated to one of his two private coaches. They endured seven consecutive days of rain in Central Mexico followed by weeks of drought in the Chihuahuan Desert. The last five days of their journey they ran out of food and water and were reduced to eating roots of desert plants and extracting water from cactus leaves until they reached El Paso del Norte, the Pass of the North, a deep chasm between two mountain ranges. They crossed the Rio Bravo, now known as the Rio Grande, on the south bank to the opposite bank at San Elizario, about fifteen miles southeast of the future El Paso, Texas. There Oñate and his weary travelers rested.

On April 28, 1598, Oñate performed the ceremony of La Toma (Taking Possession), claiming the province Nuevo Mexico for his King Philip II. The travelers gave thanks with a Mass and feast. "We built a great bonfire and roasted the meat and fish. . . . we were happy that our trials were over; as happy as were the passengers in the Ark when they saw the dove returning with the olive branch in his beak, bringing tidings that the deluge had subsided," wrote a member of the expedition.

Their trials were not over. Proceeding north, the colonists caravanned through hard terrain along a rough trail, often no more than a burro track, a route that would become the *Camino Real* (Royal Road) extending from Nueva Vizcaya in Mexico to northern New Mexico. Not far from the San Juan Pueblo (Ohkay Owingeh), about thirty miles from Santa Fe, Oñate established his headquarters for the province of New Mexico.

The Spanish colonists migrated to stay and forge a new life. Some hoped to find gold and silver while others were content to harness precious water from the Rio Grande to irrigate the temperamental wheat crop. In the fields and mines the Puebloans labored for the Spanish. The friars built thick walls around the mission complex dominated by an adobe church with massive floor-to-roof buttresses. Within sight of the terraced Pueblo apartment houses accessed through trapdoors in the roof, the homesteader sunbaked adobe bricks and laid one-story freestanding houses with windows and heavy wood doors.

Behind a few of the closed doors, away from the prying eyes of their neighbors, the Sephardic families sat at the table for Passover Seder and might have broken corn tortillas instead of matzoh, unavailable on the frontier. "Since the tortillas do not have leavening and corn is not one of the grains forbidden by the Sephardic tradition, they might have eaten tortillas. According to the strictest interpretation of Jewish Law as accepted today, tortillas would not be allowed but there were no rabbinical authorities to oversee those communities," says Rabbi Arnold Mark Belzer.

In the backyard of their homes the colonists constructed the Spanish *horno*, a beehive-shaped, domed adobe oven for baking

Adobe home with horno, *Spanish outdoor oven, around 1900 in Santa Fe, New Mexico. (Courtesy of New Mexico State University Library, Archives and Special Collections, Las Cruces, New Mexico)*

bread. Early in the morning the housewife built a fire inside the thick adobe chamber of the oven and closed the door. In the kitchen, she mixed wheat flour milled by the local mill, kneaded the dough, and covered it to rise while she attended to her other chores. A couple of hours later when the fire burned out, she swept clean the oven floor, placed the round loaves of dough around the hot bricks, sealed the smoke hole and doorway, and baked bread.

Wherever the Spanish put down roots, they distributed wheat seeds and planted wheat. So it was in Pueblo country the native women learned to bake bread Spanish style for the mistress of the colonial household they served. The men grew wheat for market . . . with a brief interruption by the Pueblo Revolt in 1680.

Over the years the Spanish missions demanded labor and tributes from the Puebloans and the priests condemned the native ceremonial kivas. Spanish cattle trampled Pueblo cornfields and a prolonged drought, perhaps the wrath of the gods, withered crops dependent on rainwater irrigation. And some of their own people forgot the ancient ways, the Puebloans lamented.

On August 14, 1680, more than five hundred Pueblo warriors, led by Popé of San Juan Pueblo, hovered outside the capital of Santa Fe, poised for battle to take back their land and religion. On the march the rebels murdered Franciscan missionaries and Spanish colonists, burned homes, torched wheat fields, and vandalized the shacks of indigenous Mexicans who served the Spanish. In Santa Fe, the Pueblo ignored pleas for restraint from Governor Antonio de Otermín, who was astonished at the audacity of the Puebloans. Fight or leave, the Puebloans said. Emboldened by reinforcements from sympathetic neighboring tribes, the Pueblo force seized the city, rang the bells of the San Miguel Mission, and then set fire to the church. On August 21, trapped without food and water in the government compound around the Plaza, the colonists decided to fight their way out of an untenable predicament. The skirmish was brief. Beleaguered and frightened settlers and a small group of Tigua Indians, some of them slaves, withdrew and retreated across the mountains south to El Paso del Norte.

For a time, in parts of the Pueblo region, the tribal people obliterated anything Spanish. They burned the mission churches, dismantled the remains of the charred framework, and planted corn on the church grounds. They annulled Catholic marriages and built kivas on top of demolished convents. They refused to plant wheat and, brick by brick, tore down the outdoor bread ovens. They made breechcloths out of European men's trousers. They decorated their kachina masks, performed sacred dances, and ate corn tortillas, corn breads, corn gruel, corn stews, and roasted corn. For a time.

In 1692 the loose-knit Pueblo union fell apart. Seizing the window of opportunity, Diego de Vargas and rejuvenated Spanish forces marched into Santa Fe and reclaimed the province of New Mexico.

The Upper Pima

In the Upper Pima (Pimería Alta) region of the northern state of Sonora, Mexico, and southern Arizona, it was Jesuit country. The Jesuit mission system was a complex economic and religious institution of Spanish colonialism to solidify the tenuous Spanish presence on the frontier. While the Jesuits intended to convert the natives to the Roman Catholic faith, the Spanish crown expected the missions to accrue income and resources necessary for self-sufficiency. Thus, the padres built churches, established farms, and conducted trade.

The frontier missions primarily survived with communal agriculture and the labor force of the indigenous people working "for the Father whom they hope to receive." During the work week, six days at the peak of planting and harvesting, the laborers farmed the communal fields and tended livestock. The missionaries paid them with spiritual teaching, seeds for their family plot, and supplemental food, usually European— beef jerky and bread. They received medicine, smoking tobacco, and respectable Spanish clothing—trousers for the men and long skirts for the women topped with a tunic called a tilma.

In 1687 King Philip V sent Father Eusebio Francisco Kino to the Upper Pima. For twenty-four years, Kino crisscrossed fertile river valleys, low mountains, and desolate desert country to oversee the missions. From his home mission of Nuestra Señora de los Dolores in northernmost Sonora, Kino mounted his horse, slid his boots into the stirrups, draped his black cassock over the saddle, and pulled up his hood to shield the sun. He carried wheat seeds in a weatherproof supply pouch made from leftover scraps of coarse fabric used to repair Spanish ship sails. He tucked a Bible, gold chalice, and the liturgical white robe and stole into a leather saddlebag. For emergencies he packed dried tortillas. Should he meet an itinerant traveler in between mission settlements he would stop, say Mass, and bless the communion tortilla.

Pimería Alta missions map around the time of Father Kino. (Tom Wilbur; redrawn from Tumacacori's Yesterdays, U.S. Department of the Interior, National Park Service)

Kino and his small entourage of native servants—including
an occasional ranch hand or sometimes a visiting Jesuit col-
league, but almost never a military escort—journeyed hundreds
of miles, covering thirty or more miles a day. He explored,
mapped, converted, built churches, traded, stocked mission
lands with large herds of cattle, and promoted wheat and European farming techniques.

Kino was pleased with the economic prosperity and the converted "docile and industrious Indians" of the Jesuit missions
in Sonora. "More than forty boys came forth to receive us with
their crosses in their hands, and there were more than three
hundred Indians drawn up in a line. . . . Afterward we counted
more than a thousand souls. There were an earth-roofed adobe
house, cattle, sheep and goats, wheat and maize. We killed three
beeves and two sheep. The fields and lands for sowing were so
extensive and supplied with so many irrigation ditches running
along the ground that the father visitor said they were sufficient
for another city like Mexico."

Fr. Kino was not quite so pleased with the scattered mission
outposts straddling the border of southeastern Arizona and
northwest Mexico. Here in the Sonoran Desert, the Tohono
O'odham lived, the "desert people." Scarred by rebellions and
largely understaffed without a resident priest, the missions
were disorganized and the indoctrination of Catholic rituals
and beliefs faltered. Nonetheless, Kino spread the word of the
Jesuit through good works, introducing livestock and distribut-
ing wheat seeds. Wheat and the consequent wheat flour tortilla
were so successful the descendants of the Tohono O'odham
do not recall their grandparents talking about or making corn
tortillas.

Wheat, Kino noted, could be farmed during the spring and
summer, dependent on summer monsoon deluges for water, and
harvested in the fall. During the mild winter in the Upper Pima
region, the fields lay fallow. Yet in his Mediterranean homeland
the farmers grew wheat as a winter crop, planted during the

rainy cool season and harvested during the summer dry season. Wheat was fickle. In Central Mexico where the Spaniards depended on the wheat crop for their supply of bread, summer was a brutal time for wheat. It tolerated the high altitude of Mexico's plateaus, but in the high humidity, heat, and torrential downpours of summer, its leaves rusted and reduced the yield. How well the Mexico City residents remembered the wheat catastrophe of 1602 when the desperate colonists broke down and ate corn tortillas.

But in northern Sonora, Mexico, and parts of the southwest Upper Pima, light rains, *equipata* rains, fell in the mild winter. So why not plant winter wheat? Wheat planted in October matured during the warm days and cool nights and was ready for harvest in May, adding a second growing season to supplement corn, beans, and squash, all sun-loving summer crops. Thus, the Jesuits, the colonists, and the indigenous people planted a lot of winter wheat.

Across the Atlantic Ocean in the Spanish court, the King of Spain recognized the economic advantage of a steady supply of market wheat and sent a new wave of land owners, merchants, and millers to Sonora. In time, farmers sold bumper crops of wheat to all of Mexico including the Pacific coast and to parts of the Southwest.

In the mission kitchen, the native servants ground the wheat seeds on the traditional stone metate reserved for corn—until mule-powered gristmills replaced hand labor. Over time, small farmstead mills in Sonora became obsolete and grain bins taller than churches shadowed local town mills. Fed by the bountiful wheat harvests, flour mills operated twenty-four hours a day to grind wheat grain into flour.

At the mission altar the Jesuit priest, conscience clear, broke communion bread, this time the leavened bread of the Holy Eucharist instead of the poor substitute, bits of dried corn tortilla or moldy bread.

In the silver and mining communities the miners melted

pieces of metal in lieu of coins, unavailable in the northern frontier, and bought bread made in the Jesuit kitchens.

On the large, land-grant haciendas the Spanish *patrón*, usually at odds with the Jesuits because the missions profited from the most desirable farmlands and cheap indigenous labor, conceded that winter wheat was a brilliant crop innovation and converted some of his precious stock land to cultivation.

In Sonora, the pragmatic Norteño (Northerner)—rough-and-ready pioneer criollos of Spanish descent and mestizos, the changing order of Spanish blood mixed with Indio—shifted from the traditional corn-based culture to the new wheat culture. The wheat grew and the people prospered. "In Sonora being modern has been a preferred mode of being since the 18th century," says anthropologist Maribel Alvarez. Physically distant from the authorities in Mexico City and coping with a harsh

---

Mexican Cookbook

This recipe for flour tortillas was popular in New Mexico when the province was part of the Republic of Mexico. It was taken from *Mexican Cookbook* published in 1945 by Erna Fergusson, courtesy of the University of New Mexico Press.

Tortillas (with wheat flour)

2 cups flour
1 teaspoon salt
1½ teaspoon baking powder
1 tablespoon fat
cold water

Mix and sift dry ingredients, cut in the fat and add cold water to make a stiff dough, ⅔ cup. Knead on lightly floured board, make small balls, pat thin, bake on soapstone or lightly greased griddle.

Men cooking tortillas in Juárez, Mexico, early 1900s. (Courtesy of El Paso County Historical Society, El Paso, Texas)

environment and roaming warrior tribes, Sonorans considered themselves economically and politically miles apart from mainstream Mexico. They were borderlanders who survived by being open to new ideas and technologies and different cultures.

Tortilla de Harina, the Wheat Flour Tortilla

A distinctive feature of the northern frontier was the wheat flour tortilla. On Spanish ranches, in colonial settlements, and even in indigenous communities, mining villages, cities, and border towns, the women mixed locally milled White Sonora wheat flour with water, salt, and lard rendered from swine, a divergence from the traditional vegetarian corn tortilla. Instead of kneeling before the metate to grind corn, the women bent from the waist to knead the dough and divide it into small balls. They rolled each ball into a thin white wheat flour tortilla, *tortilla de harina*, stretching the tortilla to fourteen, sixteen, or eighteen inches in diameter, the *tortilla grande de harina*. And now the men participated and learned the art of stretching the dough to a large thin tortilla or a thicker, smaller eight-inch tortilla. Cooked on a griddle, often the traditional comal, and rolled around a mound of signature Sonora grilled beef, the Sonora tortilla transformed into today's worldly cross-cultural burrito.

GUEST ESSAY

• • • • •

Sonoran Flour Tortillas
What's in a Name?

MARIBEL ALVAREZ, UNIVERSITY OF ARIZONA

In Sonora, Mexico, the curious word *sobaquera* is frequently used to refer to the extra-large wheat flour tortillas that are prepared and consumed in the northern regions of the country. Despite the popularity of the term, significant controversy exists among Sonorenses about the origins and desirability of the term. Step into the bustling municipal market or stop by any roadside food stand and you will hear ordinary working-class Sonorans utilizing the word liberally. Bring up the term, however, among the educated and the elite and you risk a severe admonition about the pejorative and prejudicial implications attached to one of the state's most iconic foodways. The preferred appellative is *tortilla de agua* (water-based flour tortilla). The disdain for the term *sobaquera* derives partly from the association with the word *sobaco* (street slang for armpit). One interpretation posits that the movement required to stretch the dough in order to produce the large, paper-thin tortilla goes beyond the tortilla maker's hands all the way to her arm and shoulder—more specifically, the Sonoran flour tortilla demands a kind of sweeping motion that exposes the maker's armpit over the comal or stove. For some, however, the armpit (especially its vulgar street name) is associated with a lack of hygiene. It is widely believed that the Mexican TV animator Raúl Velasco (an Ed Sullivan–like presenter) coined the term when he traveled to Sonora to film a special segment for his highly popular Sunday variety show "Siempre en Domingo" sometime in the early 1980s. Sonorans have always embraced a strong and proud regional identity, particularly vis-à-vis the cultural and political hegemony of Central Mexico. Many in Sonora find it all too predictable and biased that a Central Mexican figure would have named with a term of vulgarity one of the state's most valued culinary traditions. There is another possible explanation for the term *sobaquera* that has little to do with these culture wars. A sobaquera is also a Spanish term for a leather bag or holster. Some believe that the word became attached to tortillas as early as the 1700s when travel on horse across Sonora's rugged rural terrain required that the early cowboys carry along nourishment to last for several days. The large bread substitutes were folded easily and carried in the sobaqueras alongside guns and beef jerky (*carne seca*), another Sonoran delicacy.

• • • • •

Was the wheat flour tortilla a regional adaptation of the corn tortilla? Wheat culture alone does not explain the origin of the flour tortilla, for people grew wheat in Central Mexico and made bread instead of flour tortillas. Or was the wheat flour tortilla a form of Middle Eastern flatbread influenced by the Moslem and Sephardic settlers in northern Mexico and New Mexico? These are intriguing theories, but a definitive origin is difficult to trace.

For sure, wheat competed with corn as the dominant crop, and the northern frontier people—a cultural and geographical region composed of present-day Sonora, Chihuahua, southeastern Arizona, and southern New Mexico—identified with the flour tortilla. Mexicans in Central Mexico continued to prefer the corn tortilla because they liked the taste, corn was easy and inexpensive to grow in small home plots, and the corn tortilla symbolized their regional and national pride. But in Sonora and northern Mexico, by the beginning of the nineteenth century the flour tortilla evolved into the major tortilla consumed daily and in fiestas, following the fortunes of Spain to Spanish Texas and California, and then the misfortunes of Spain to independent Texas and California.

Chapter 5

• • • THE FRONTIER TORTILLA

In the 1500s wayward groups of free-range Corriente cattle, a hardy breed of the original Spanish cattle brought to the New World able to withstand the ocean crossing and adapt to the Americas, wandered north from the haciendas in Central Mexico to El Paso del Norte. The cattle drank from the Rio Grande and spread through the upper and lower river valleys, stretching their necks to reach the lower leaves of cottonwood trees growing along the banks and chewing on shrubs and tall grasses. Then the Mexican colonists came, lured by frontier dreams of wide-open land, floodwater irrigation, and a bit of New World independence from the Old World class society transported by elite Spaniards to New Spain.

The El Paso province—the site of two future border cities, Ciudad Juárez on the Mexican side and El Paso on the Texas side—comprised one of four colonial provinces in the small piece of modern Texas occupied by the Spanish and then independent Mexico. By the 1700s sparse settlements grew large, and the Spanish-speaking colonists named towns, cities, counties, mountains, and rivers. They planted European wheat and raised cattle, sheep, goats, and swine. In the courtroom they argued land and water regulations and family law. In San Antonio they built the "Queen of Missions," San José y San Miguel de Aguayo, an imposing complex of stone walls, bastions, granary, and a grand church. They sang "Corrido de los oprimidos," the ballad of the oppressed, to celebrate the Mexican War of Independence. They inspired the popularity of the wheat flour tortilla. Mexico came to Texas.

San Elizario, fifteen miles southeast of El Paso, was typical of the Texas towns that grew up around Spanish missions and presidios (garrisons) along the Rio Grande. Tied to their Spanish ways, the farmers planted their primary crop of wheat in long rows, *porciónes*, bordered by the Rio Grande and irrigated by community ditches called *acequias*. The close-knit families were devout Catholics united by their Spanish heritage. On Sundays they went to church, La Capilla de San Elcear in the Plaza. They lived in low, hacienda-style homes made of sun-dried adobe bricks, often fortified with chicken and other animal bones. Cottonwood vigas (beams) supported flat roofs. The wealthier the family, the bigger the house. Each night they locked the heavy wooden gate inset in an adobe wall surrounding the house, walling out Apache raiders. On the outskirts of town in the desert foothills the rural poor, among them Hispanized Texas Indians, lived in one-room straw-thatched jacales made of mesquite poles chinked with mud or adobe.

"My maternal great-grandmother Refugio (Cuca) Aldana Aranda came to San Elizario, Texas, from Aguascalientes, Mexico. In Mexico, she was married to a well-to-do man but he gambled and drank away his inheritance from the family silver mines. He even bet his wife Cuca, my great-grandmother, and his daughter Anita, my grandmother, in a poker game. He lost, and Cuca separated from him, breaking his bet. He proceeded to drink himself to death at the ripe old age of thirty-four," says Lillian Trujillo, a sixth-generation San Elizario resident.

Friends followed friends, and Cuca and her daughter immigrated to San Elizario, Texas, where people from home welcomed them. There Cuca married Jesus Cobos, a wealthy widower, and set up housekeeping in his nineteenth-century rambling adobe homestead, a house she inherited along with one-half of his considerable property. The other twelve children from her husband's first marriage inherited the other half, split among them.

The original Hispanic citizens of San Elizario migrated from the interior of Mexican New Spain with Spanish surnames reminiscent of conquistadores, early colonizers, or towns and regions in Spain. We are Spanish, they proclaimed, but many were mixed race born in Mexico of Spanish heritage and intermarried with the indigenous people. This dynamic hybrid of Mexicans, called mestizo, outnumbered the full-blooded Spaniards ensconced on large ranching estates. The mestizo acquired social and economic status as cash crop framers, merchants, salt traders, millers, and growers of Elizario wine grapes. Yet "we should not romanticize this society as equalitarian," says historian Rodolfo Acuña. "Although there was diversity, race established privilege, and the more Spanish the subject appeared, the more privileges."

The tortilla culture split the racial and social divide down the middle in San Elizario. Tortillas carried meaning. As part of the northern frontier wheat culture, the established Mexican colonists adopted the wheat flour tortilla, a visible connection to their Spanish heritage and regional identity. Most significant, flour tortillas made from wheat grown by the northern colonists and ground into flour at the mill were easier and faster to prepare than working through the nixtamal process to make the corn tortilla. As part of the indigenous corn culture, the Tigua, a Puebloan tribe that fled the Pueblo Revolt in 1680 to settle in the El Paso area, continued to plant a lot of corn, higher in yields and easier to grow than wheat. A present-day tribal member tells of his great-grandmother grinding nixtamalized corn into dough, masa, the "old way" with a metate and mano. From the masa the women made corn tortillas, an indigenous food that set them apart from the northern Mexican society. "Corn tortillas were made by Indians, not Mexicans. Mexicans made flour tortillas," says Lillian Trujillo. "Tortillas were cooked by both of my grandmothers on a daily basis and all my aunts and mom also used to make them. Flour tortillas were made three times a day because they preferred them warm. They are delicious with melted butter."

Sopaipillas

Sopaipillas are made from the wheat flour tortilla, a sweet version to finish a fiery Mexican meal. This recipe is courtesy of the *San Elizario Genealogy and Historical Society Cookbook,* San Elizario, Texas. Lillian Trujillo, a sixth-generation descendent of Spanish immigrants from Mexico, talked to three different members about the recipe. "They all say you roll out the dough the same way as tortillas, but thicker. The shortening can be lard. Cut into triangles, then fry until it puffs up. Serve with honey for dipping, or for a different taste, boil cinnamon sticks in water and use instead of regular water to get a cinnamon flavor sopaipilla."

    4 cups flour
    milk/water, as needed
    1 teaspoon salt
    2 cups frying oil
    2 teaspoons baking powder
    ½ cup sugar
    2 tablespoons shortening
    1 teaspoon ground cinnamon

Sift together flour, salt and baking powder. Add shortening. Add enough milk or water to make a medium dough, not stiff. Let dough stand for 30 minutes, covered. Roll out ¼-inch thick and cut into 4s. Fry in deep oil (HOT) until brown and puffed up. Combine sugar and cinnamon. Sprinkle on sopaipillas while they are draining and still hot.

The Salt War

In the late nineteenth century, the San Elizario housewife did not have to go far to buy a bag of flour to make her tortillas. On Main Street, Charles Ellis and his Hispanic wife Teodora Alarcon operated the grist and roller mill where they ground wheat into flour . . . until an armed mob chased and caught Ellis, tied his feet in the stirrups of a horse, dragged him through town until dead, and then slit his throat. Ellis was the collateral victim of a political feud that took on a racial cast between the large population of Mexicans and Mexican-Americans, stereotyped as the tortilla people, and the "Boss Rule" of second- or third-generation Northern Europeans, known as Anglos.

It was 1877 and Texas was part of the United States. The Salt War, a simmering political dispute over the rights of salt deposits in the Guadalupe Mountains east of El Paso, took place in the racial and ethnic borderlands between Texas and northern Mexico. It culminated in a blaze of gun fire in San Elizario.

Were the salt lakes undeeded public lands, traditionally a source of free salt for communal use? Or did private investors acquire the right to own the salt lakes? Anglo Texan political bosses courted votes, attorneys connived, and neighbors feuded. Groups of ethnic Mexicans on both sides of the Rio Grande joined political forces because they suspected that local politicians and legalists changed the rules in favor of private ownership to benefit their own interests. The overwhelmingly Mexican residents in the border towns, on the other hand, considered the salt lake public property, just as it was before the United States acquired Texas and split Mexico down the middle of the Rio Grande.

Ultimately, the conflict escalated into a bloody siege in San Elizario. Sympathizers on both sides were wounded and killed, stores looted, wheat crops lost, and the Texas Rangers chased the mob leaders for free salt across the Rio Grande to Mexico. The salt rights converted to private ownership.

Mexican Texas

Before there was the United States Texas there was Mexican Texas. In 1821 the Spanish colonial empire in Mexico collapsed, and after three hundred years of Spanish domination, Mexico declared independence.

Struggling with debt, poor infrastructure, and inexperienced self-rule, Mexico chose a novel, and ultimately self-defeating, idea to vitalize its remote and huge northern frontier of Texas. The

Mexican government invited settlers from the United States to cross the border into Texas where millions of acres of land awaited them to farm and ranch . . . if there was water, an issue omitted by the promoters. In return for land, the newcomers swore allegiance to Mexico and the Catholic faith. Some lied, others grabbed land for speculation. But many of the Anglos simply wanted to homestead because this was the American dream, a new life in a new land. Thus, the door opened and the newcomers infiltrated in and around insular Mexican towns like San Elizario on the border of New Spain's former North American empire.

The basic structure of Hispanic society and economy remained but the demographics shifted. How did the Hispanics adjust to the new settlers? They formed a pocket of the long-standing Mexican culture within the expanding community of different religions, classes, and ethnicities, and kept their identity alive with traditions that included warm tortillas at mealtimes.

U.S. Texas

By 1836 Texas broke off from Mexico and declared the Republic of Texas. Twelve years later in 1848, the Treaty of Guadalupe Hidalgo ended the U.S.-Mexican War, a war the United States won militarily and politically, and Texas joined the United States. Mexico's territorial loss was the U.S.'s gain of over five hundred thousand square miles of valuable land. It was the responsibility of the United States to expand across the continent and spread the benefits of democracy. Or so the proponents of Manifest Destiny claimed.

The ordinary Texas Mexicans were not interested in the moral justification of the treaty negotiations. They wanted to retain their land and be included as part of the future and governance of Texas. They wanted to be accepted as American or Mexican American or Tejano (a Texan of Mexican descent). They wanted their rights protected in practice as well as theory. They had one year to choose to return to Mexico or remain in Texas.

Most of them stayed because Texas was their home. Those who lost their land, because they misunderstood the registration rules or an unscrupulous newcomer exploited the land rights mess, felt reduced to second-class citizens. This time the shift of power interrupted the continuity of key Hispanic landholders, merchants, civic leaders, and politicians. The Hispanics shared the Southwest frontier with the Euro-Americans who viewed the tortilla culture with a mixture of often-reciprocated suspicion and tenuous respect.

The Westward Movement in the 1800s

"Mattie has a little Mexican boy that she plays with and is learning Spanish very fast," said Charles Brown, who moved his family from Virginia to a small, one-story adobe home with windows barely larger than slits, about a mile from the Rio Grande on the New Mexico border. In 1884, his wife Maggie Brown wrote home to relatives who read her letters from the elegant drawing room of a two-story antebellum house in Virginia. "If we don't know what they say I just call Mattie up & she can nearly always tell me & when she is playing with the little boy she talks it all together."

For Maggie Brown's six-year-old daughter, the Mexican children were her friends. But for the newcomers like class-conscious Maggie, the Mexicans, not the Anglo settlers, were the foreigners. She admitted her Mexican neighbors were "quiet, orderly, law-abiding, frugal people." Still, they spoke Spanish and they were Catholic, not Protestant, and they ate strange food and fiery chiles. Though Charles Brown bragged, "By the way, you ought to see us eat red pepper. I eat about 6 or 8 pods at a meal and don't think anything of it, am very fond of it."

By then on the Southwestern frontier, Mexicans, Mexican Americans, Anglos, and even the indigenous people who liked the taste of lard ate wheat flour tortillas. For a few minutes, the time it took to bite into a warm tortilla stuffed with meat smothered with green chile sauce, a dirt-poor farm laborer or a cattle baron, a Hispanic merchant or a schoolteacher from Philadelphia, a cowboy on the range or a forty-niner on the road to California were equal.

California

At the time, thousands of settlers from every state of the American union were on the move to California, one more desirable piece of territory acquired from Mexico by the United States in the Treaty of Guadalupe Hidalgo. When the Westward wagon trains followed the southern desert route, they crossed southwestern Texas. Some days the train covered twelve miles; other days one mile. The labyrinth of trails, known as part of the Ox Bow Route of the Butterfield Overland Stage, twisted and diverged through harsh country. Alkaline waters poisoned livestock. Yet better hot than cold, the travelers thought, and the land was flatter than the shorter northern route.

The families traveled in wagons constructed of forest hardwoods like hickory, oak, or maple and led by strong oxen pulling up to several thousand pounds of supplies. They packed ample gunpowder, rope, flour, and sugar, but the women missed picking produce from their kitchen gardens and collecting eggs from the barnyard chickens. "Passed through Fort Davis (Texas) . . . The valley is wide here and the mountains small. Here are found vegetables. Very high (price), roasting ears one dollar and 50 cents per dozen, butter one dollar per pound, eggs the same per dozen," wrote Harriet Bunyard in 1869. But the native tortillas were cheap, filling, and tasted almost as good as bread. At each stopping point in an isolated border village the frontier women bartered for fresh, hot burritos from the burrito lady and wrapped a few extra in a towel and stuck them in a leather packet for the next day on the trail.

The new settlers overwhelmed the Californios, the Spanish-speaking Californians from colonial Mexico. In Spanish

California, as in Spanish Texas, many of the New Spain settlers were racially mixed mestizo. Far from the authority of Mexico City, the Californio elite—the wealthy landed gentry—ignored the mestizo caste label. "We are the *gente de razón*" (the people of reason), they claimed. Politically, culturally, and socially, they distanced themselves from the lower end of Californio society— convicts banished to California by the Mexican government, the unwanted Indios, and the poorly educated Mexicans toiling in the fields or mines.

To the California Anglos, Mexicans were Mexicans, all classes categorized as one. One label was easier to assign than figuring out who was mestizo, Indio, hidalgo (minor nobility), or full-blooded Spanish. So the gente de razón could not use their cultural identity to their benefit. Amid a climate of racial denigration and conflicts between populations, they lost their favored status and political dominance. For a particularly vocal segment of the new Anglo majority, the beef burrito, an acculturation food of the frontier, was the only aspect of the Mexican culture welcome in California.

Encarnación's Cookbook

In California, land was as golden as the mineral and the new settlers wanted what the gente de razón possessed: land and the power that accompanied it. Sometimes an Anglo married a land-rich, light-complexioned rancher's daughter. Or the land office reversed or lost Spanish land titles and the newcomers stepped in. Or racist groups questioned a Californio's loyalty, jailed him, and confiscated his property. And sometimes vigilantes killed.

One of the earliest Californio settlers of northern California was Nicolás Antonio Berreyesa, who immigrated to California from Mexico with the Juan Bautista de Anza expedition in 1775. The Berreyesa family rose to prominence and then fell to personal tragedies and land-litigation setbacks.

How could the Berreyesas forget and forgive Indian fighter

Kit Carson, who gunned down José de los Reyes Berreyesa, a sixty-one year old civilized gentleman? Yet it happened in 1846 when California was part of Mexico and Bear Flag rebels bristled to break away from Mexico. The rebels saw Mexican enemies everywhere. As José and his two nephews rowed ashore in San Francisco Bay, a group of rebels sounded the alarm: Mexican spies! And they shot and killed the two young men. The bereft José threw himself on the slain bodies. Then Kit Carson shot José too.

How could the Berreyesas forget the lynching? In 1854 a lynch mob hung José's son over a dispute about the New Almaden Mine, a rich mercury deposit on the Berreyesa land. And what about the loss of thousands of acres of ranchland? The family remembered.

Into this proud family Lorenzo and María del Carmen Berreyesa Pinedo brought a daughter, Encarnación Pinedo, born May 1848. Fifty years later, Encarnación, a spinster, asserted her Californio legacy through food. In 1898 she wrote a cookbook, the first cookbook written by a Hispanic in the United States and largely unknown until translated by culinary historian Dan Strehl in 2003.

Encarnación wrote *The Spanish Cook: A Work Containing a Thousand Valuable and Useful Recipes to Cook with Ease in Different Styles, Including Advice and Explanations That Put the Art of Cooking within Reach of Everyone* (*El cocinero español: Obra que contiene mil recetas valiosas y utiles para cocinar con facilidad en diferentes estilos. Comprendido advertencias y explicaciones aproposito que ponen el arte de la cocina al alcance de todos*). At the time, her publisher was quite bold to present a book in Spanish about Mexican cuisine authored by a Californio woman.

In her kitchen Encarnación prepared corn tortillas the nixtamal way, a tradition preserved by immigrant colonists from Central Mexico. "Add two tbsp strong lime and enough water to a quart of dried corn kernels. Simmer the corn, and if the skin doesn't slip, add more lime . . . then grind the corn for dough

Enterprise nixtamal
cornmill from the late
nineteenth century
manufactured by
Enterprise Manu-
facturing Company,
Philadelphia, Pennsyl-
vania. (Courtesy
of Dan Strehl)

"ENTERPRISE"
Nixtamal or Combination Mills

NIXTAMAL is a corn food product largely used
in Mexico, and this mill was primarily designed
for grinding the corn so used.

Our development has shown many other pur-
poses where the mill can be used with great advantage, such as grinding cereals, cocoa beans, vanilla
beans, poppy seed, peanuts (for peanut butter),
white lead, massage cream ingredients and for re-
ducing other materials to pasty substances.

Very adaptable for druggists' use in grinding
rosin, ginseng root, herbs, dried berries, pumice
stone, coal, etc.

This Nixtamal Mill has the advantage that the
cylinder is octagon, which permits the inside screw
to get hold of the corn in a most effective way. Of
the two knives which make up the mill, one is fastened to the machine by
three screws. When the two knives are worn out they can easily be renewed,
which makes the machine practically as good as new.

All parts are double tinned, which prevents the "masa" from becoming
discolored and also prevents the machine from rusting. The hopper or
receptacle is of cast iron, made in one single piece, which permits the
operator to exert a pressure on the corn with the free hand.

HAND MILLS AS ABOVE ILLUSTRATED   Prices

No. 54, Weight, 6 pounds; Capacity, 2 pounds per minute, $1.75
No. 64, Weight, 12 pounds; Capacity, 3 pounds per minute, 3.50
         Packed 6 in a case
No. 74, Weight, 24 pounds; Capacity, 5 pounds per minute, 7.50
         Packed 1 in a case

and tortillas." But Encarnación was from the upper class, a modern cook open to new technology that saved work and time.
"There are new Enterprise machines for grinding corn that are
excellent and are superior to all others and do more than the old
Mexican *metate*," she advised her readers.

Encarnación was traditional, describing a stew made with
the penetrating red of Mexican chiles, "*Manchamanteles*, Stew that
Stains the Tablecloth." She was sardonic, calling the Anglo typical breakfast, "*Huevos Hipócritas (con jamón)*, Hypocrites' eggs with
ham." She was a serious cook, including recipes from Hispanic,
French, and Italian cuisine. She excluded what she labeled Yan-
kee food and introduced the Californio tradition through her
family's recipes. The names were Spanish—"*Tortillas de harina a la
española*, Spanish-style flour tortillas"—but the culture was California Mexican.

Since Encarnación wrote *The Spanish Cook* in Spanish, her English-
language neighbors did not read it. The separation between the
two cultures was wide, and Encarnación's cultured Californio
traditions were overshadowed by the image of the backward

and poor, lower-class Mexican—an image not only accepted in the United States but also in Porfirian Mexico.

Tortilla Bashing

At the time Encarnación was testing and compiling Mexican recipes, across the border Mexico's President Porfirio Díaz bashed the urban poor, the rural poor, the barefooted indigenous, Day of the Dead rituals, turkey flocks driven through city streets, the wooden one-handled Mexican plow, and the corn tortilla ensconced in the heart of traditional Mexico.

For thirty-five years, from 1876 until 1911, Díaz dictated his bureaucratic solutions for a progressive Mexico. Although he stabilized the constitutional government—before his regime presidents changed almost weekly—and initiated programs to build fifteen thousand miles of railroad and to promote foreign investment in transportation, mines, manufacture, and agriculture, he exacerbated the split between rich and poor. Díaz liked wealth and technology and European fashion and French cuisine with champagne. It was said that when it rained in London, Díaz unfolded his umbrella and made his rounds under sunny Mexican skies.

In the presidential office, Díaz listened to Senator Francisco Bulnes theorize why Mexico lagged behind the United States. In an event described as the "tortilla discourse" by historian Jeffrey Pilcher, Bulnes pontificated about the indigenous people outside the mainstream of the market economy and Porfirian nationalism. They were nutritionally weak, too poor and backward and inhibited by the past to be productive or motivated, he said. Three times a day, every day, they ate tortillas and tamales and drank atole—all made from corn. They should eat bread and meat.

Based on dubious nutritional science, Bulnes and his supporters divided civilized humans into three races: the people of corn, wheat, and rice. They looked across the Atlantic Ocean to Europe and north to the United States, where the wheat people ate bread and developed modern industrial societies. And then they stepped outside their grand Mexico City and looked around the countryside, where the indigenous housewife ground corn for tortillas on a stone metate and her husband used a horn spoon for a shovel and a piece of rawhide stretched between two poles for a wheelbarrow. Ignoring urgent issues of poor education and social inequalities, food crises and land reform, Díaz attacked corn and the lifestyle and customs associated with corn in the name of progress.

The majority of ordinary Mexicans identified with the corn tortilla, gathering strength from it as a food and cultural tradition preserving the legacy of Mesoamerican civilizations. They ignored the Porfirian elite and ate enchiladas at the Lady of Guadalupe Festival and stood in line to buy tortillas wrapped around grilled pork from street vendors. Soon Díaz was gone, overthrown in 1911 by revolutionary insurgents, and tortilla patriotism replaced tortilla bashing.

The Soldadera

Between 1910 and 1920, approximately 900,000 Mexicans lost their lives in the Mexican Revolution and more than 890,000 documented Mexican immigrants found refuge in the United States. It began in 1910 when determined groups of excluded and dominated working- and middle-class reformers allied themselves with the peasant class and went to war. The revolution stormed through Mexico with a nationalistic vision for a fairer life. "It is better to die on your feet than to live on your knees," said rebel leader Emiliano Zapata. While Zapata led the troops in the south, Pascual Orozco and Francisco "Pancho" Villa entrenched their armies in the north.

Following the Mexican troops were the soldaderas. They were the women who carried baskets of food and clothes and loaded cooking pots and chickens in a cage on the transport train or the

(above) Camp family cooking tortillas, early 1900s. (Courtesy of El Paso County Historical Society, El Paso, Texas)

(left) Las soldaderas, the women of the Mexican Revolution, 1910–1920. (Courtesy of Nettie Lee Benson Latin American Collection, University of Texas Libraries, University of Texas at Austin)

back of a burro. Sometimes their children accompanied them. The women hauled firewood and water and ground corn on the stone metate they brought from home to make tortillas. On the battlefield they carried food, water, and ammunition, bandaged the wounded, and looted the enemy dead for valuables passed on to the soldiers.

The soldadera could be the young wife so in love she did not want to be parted from her husband. In the crowded box car of a troop train she created the home hearth, or in peaceful moments, filled a vase with flowers and spread a tablecloth on the ground in a vacant pasture.

Or she was the dutiful wife who told American war reporter John Reed, "I remember well when Filadelfo called to me in the little morning before it was light—we lived in Pachuca—and said: 'Come! We are going out to fight because the good Pancho Madero has been murdered this day!' . . . And I said, 'Why must I come?' And he answered, 'Shall I starve then? Who shall make my tortillas for me but my woman?'"

The soldadera could be the hungry Indio from the parched hills who willingly accompanied her husband because she knew she would always have food in the army.

Or the soldadera could be enlisted as an unsuspected female smuggler bringing guns or medicine across the border from the United States, and hiding ammunition underneath her skirt.

Some soldaderas had little choice because they were drafted as troop cooks. And others chose the role of mistress or prostitute, often traveling in dedicated train coaches.

On the battlefield the most fearless and bold of the soldaderas

Cooking for the army of the Mexican Revolution, 1910–1920. (Courtesy of El Paso County Historical Society, El Paso, Texas)

fought. "If a woman's husband was killed, she could either attach herself to some other man or take over his uniform and gun herself. Almost every troop had a famous lady colonel or lady captain, a husky, earringed girl armed to the teeth and among headlong, reckless fighters, one of the first," wrote journalist Anita Brenner. Some of the fighting rebels were rugged country women, others worldly city dwellers, and one, "La China," was a former tortilla maker. "La China" led the female contingent of angry women avenging the deaths of the Zapatista insurgents in the Puente de Ixtla Morelos region. "Some in rags, some in plundered finery, wearing silk stockings and dresses, sandals, straw hats and gun belts, these women became terrors of the region," writes historian John Womack.

The revolution ended in 1920 and the soldadera resumed her role in the Mexican home. But home was different. In areas of the countryside where there was electric power, relieved house-wives put aside their metate and carried a bucket of lime-soaked corn kernels to the mechanized corn-grinding mill. Often they incurred a dismissive shake of the head from many an elderly matriarch, or the resistance of a particularly threatened hus-band who believed "the more occupied a woman is, the less are the possibilities of infidelity." At the store, women with saved household money bought hand-operated manufactured tortilla presses to form uniformly round tortillas. And some families left their village and went to the city where the women joined the men to work in the booming factories, leaving tortilla making to the stay-at-home wife or the neighborhood tortillería.

In Mexico City, the middle-class woman who at one time shunned tortillas as peasant food, in a burst of nationalistic fever adopted corn tortillas. However, she was not about to spend her day manually making tortillas, so she bought a table-sized elec-trically powered grinding mill to grind corn in the home, pref-erably by an indigenous servant.

The market was ripe for store-bought corn tortillas, bashed

by tortilla purists, but increasingly acceptable as good enough in this period of modernization. By the late 1920s in most neighborhoods there was a tortillería, some operated in conjunction with the nixtamal cornmills and others family owned—a boon for small business entrepreneurs. Attitudes changed. The man who refused to get his hands sticky mixing corn dough at home now accepted tortilla making as a fledgling industry, an opportunity to earn money by churning out batches of tortillas on machines. Initially the traditional Mexican cook was a bit reluctant to give up her identity as "tortilla mama," but slowly the word spread—machines produced more tortillas in less time with less work.

Chapter 6

• • • THE INDUSTRIAL TORTILLA

Before dawn, Anita Hernández Lucas and her mother rose and went their separate ways to different cornmills to begin work by 3:30 in the morning. Hernández's story began in 1916 when she was born in Mexico City. Her father fought during the Mexican Revolution and her mother followed him as a soldadera from battlefield to battlefield where he died, she told historian María Teresa Fernández-Acevas. In the 1920s her mother moved the family from Mexico City to Guadalajara where they lived on a small military pension supplemented by her mother's work as a torteadora, a tortilla maker, paid piece rate for the number of tortillas produced.

At the cornmill, by six in the morning workers turned out the first batch of large quantities of masa, the nixtamalized corn dough made from wet corn grinders powered by gas engines and electric motors. At six in the evening they were still at work, for the more dough made and sold, the more money earned.

Work conditions in the molino de nixtamal (nixtamal cornmill) could be harsh, and until the late 1920s unregulated. Unskilled, poor and uneducated women accepted what was available, a take-it-or-leave-it job. Undisputed woman's work was forming dough balls or selling the dough in the shop adjoining the mill. Women competed with men for the job of nixtamalera, a person who worked alongside the men tending hot vats of simmering lime-treated corn kernels. Women hoped to prepare the lime solution, operate simple dough machines, or supervise, the best-paid skilled positions open to both men and women (but dominated by the former). Only men hauled the finished product, heavy loads of corn dough.

After work, Anita and her mother listened to the rousing speeches of women textile workers, schoolteachers, and tortilla workers, fed up with demeaning work conditions, unequal pay, and passive Mexican women. "This was stronger than the household, the home, and parents. We went to the meetings without eating, without sleeping in order to go the labor struggle; this was a full time job," said Hernández.

The Hernández women joined the budding labor movement, which initially consisted of mixed unions with men and women advocating for better paid positions, then later split into separate men's and women's organizations as the technical hierarchy of the industry grew and the men gravitated to the higher-paid, mechanized jobs. From shop worker to labor leader, Anita led six hundred unionized women working as tortilla workers in the cornmills and tortilla factories. In time, she became a labor inspector and a city council member. Her children eventually joined the family tradition as a third generation of labor organizers.

Economically disadvantaged women like Anita Hernández Lucas entered the industrialized work force, earned wages, learned to read and write, and organized labor strikes. Were the bloody strikes and boycotts, hostility, and family sacrifices worth it? There was no guarantee of complete woman's emancipation in the male-dominated tortilla industry, but take notice, Hernández and others pointed out: working-class women had rights. And they savored their important victories. For these women the tortilla, the symbol of national tradition, was also the symbol of social and economic change.

Instant Corn Flour

For scientists, inventors, dreamers, and entrepreneurs the corn tortilla offered a golden opportunity to gain a bit of fame and make a lot of money . . . if they changed the homegrown art of the pre-Hispanic hearth into a mass-produced, mass-marketed, high-technology commodity. In one year the average Mexican ate about 220 pounds of tortillas. In the central part of Mexico at least 85 percent of the population ate corn tortillas three times a day. The industrialized corn tortilla was an untapped market to exploit in Mexico.

The engineers and tinkerers went to work to solve the problems of sticky, scorched, and misshapen factory tortillas made from corn dough. Moist nixtamalized dough clogged machinery. Early tortilla presses flattened the dough with rough edges. Conveyor belts stalled, flipping tortillas on the floor or burning them. And a system of ovens had to be carefully timed and regulated to produce the perfectly cooked tortilla acceptable to the picky Mexican consumer.

Why couldn't the corn tortilla be more like the wheat flour tortilla? The wheat farmer harvested the wheat, dried it in the fields and delivered loads of wheat grains to the mill. At the mill the miller ground the grains between stone or steel wheels into flour. No wet dough to stick to the wheels.

Easy, said the housewife in northern Mexico and the street vendor in southwest Texas who bought long-lasting bags of wheat flour and made instant tortillas. Efficient and profitable, said the flour tortilla manufacturers. With relatively simple machinery, they reconstituted milled wheat flour with water, added salt and lard, rolled and stretched as thin or thick as desired, and cooked the finished product, the flour tortilla in large masses.

The solution for the corn tortilla was the invention of dehydrated nixtamalized corn flour, masa harina. The process was revolutionary. The difference was the lime-soaked corn dough passed through a specialized grinding mill and the coarse ground particles quickly dried at high temperatures before being cooled and sifted. Large particles were reground and sifted again to achieve the ideal final particle size for corn flour.

As who made the corn tortillas and how they were made changed, so did the taste of the earthy, intense corn flavor of fresh ground corn steeped in mineral lime. "It's like the difference

Two side-by-side corn grinding mills, grinding wet nixtamal into masa dough. The wet nixtamal is filled into the mill hopper using the elevator and chute positioned above each mill hopper. (Courtesy of Michael Dunn)

between making instant mashed potatoes (just add water to a cup of dry flakes) and making mashed potatoes from real potatoes. The comparison in taste and quality—well, there really is no comparison," says Fernando Ruiz who makes tortillas from freshly ground nixtamalized corn dough for New Yorkers at Tortilleria Nixtamal. Yet the explosion of the tortilla industry and the migration of the tortilla around the world coincided with the onset of masa harina, dehydrated corn flour.

The Innovators

In 1909 word spread to Mexico from San Antonio, Texas, about the local "corn king" José Bartolomé Martínez, born in Mexico and raised in Texas. He proclaimed his newest offering of corn flour. How did he process it? Did he make nixtamalized corn flour, clearly distinguished from regular cornmeal? Martínez registered the trademark corn flour label Tamalina, although no patent for the technology is attached to the U.S. Patent Office applications. Reportedly, he boasted that his mill produced up to sixty thousand pounds of Tamalina corn flour, masa harina, as well as the traditional corn dough, masa, a day. At the end of the day, stuck with excess corn dough, he made triangle-shaped tortilla chips, perfect for dipping into beans and salsa. The people of San Antonio loved his toasted tortilla chips and so did his competitors. In time, Tamalina and Martínez were forgotten, and Frito-Lay's Tostitos were the "must-have" chips.

In 1912 in Mexico, mechanical engineer Luis Romero Soto patented his technology for dehydrated nixtamalized corn flour to reduce volumes of lime-soaked corn into flour within hours. He intended to capitalize on the innovation and go into the corn flour business, but his plans stalled.

Then in 1949 in Cerralvo, Mexico, Roberto González Barrera and his father Roberto González Gutiérrez visualized success. Father and son formed a perfect match. The older Roberto was a self-taught engineer, tweaking, improvising, and improving machines. His son, Gonzáles Barrera, was the consummate salesperson, buying, selling, and making money.

The González family sold assets, borrowed money, and bought a less-than-perfect corn flour grinder and an unused old mill. In Cerralvo, Mexico, they established the first commercial nixtamalized corn flour plant in Mexico, Molinos Azteca SA (Maseca), the genesis of Gruma, today the largest corn flour and tortilla producer in the world. They labeled their new product Maseca, adapted from *masa seca*, Spanish for "dry dough" or meal. Packaged and distributed as a product of proud Mexicans, Maseca spoke for itself.

Maseca began operations in a recycled mill with forty-five employees working three shifts around the clock. The workers dried the corn outside in the sun on the plant's dock or plugged in electric fans. In one month the primitive technology produced 150 tons of Maseca nixtamalized corn flour, and González Barrera went on the road and sold the entire inventory. Sixty years later modern technology Maseca plants worldwide produced 150 tons of corn flour per minute and González Barrera was a billionaire.

Led by González Barrera, Gruma Corporation was powerful and successful. In 1977 Gruma negotiated the purchase of the Mission Foods tortilla factory in the San Fernando Valley of Los Angeles, California, and entered the U.S. tortilla market. Eventually, Gruma established an efficient distribution system to propel a network of national and international tortilla factories and flour mills. In the Gruma flagship plant in Rancho Cucamonga, California, Mission- and Guerrero-brand corn and flour tortillas rolled off state-of-the-art machines at eleven million tortillas in a twenty-four-hour period, while separate machines produced four thousand pounds of tortilla chips each hour. González Barrera was the international "Tortilla King." In August, 2012, Don Roberto, a title of respect adopted by his employees, died.

Mexico's Tortilla Basket

While González Barrera cajoled the Mexican consumers accustomed to their mothers' fresh ground corn tortillas to accept his new product, the bureaucrats at the State Food Agency and Commerce Ministry in Mexico City deliberated. How could they ensure a steady supply of the traditional corn tortillas at stable, affordable prices? They wanted no repeat of the tortilla riots of 1943 when the corn crop failed, the cornmills closed, the tortillerías emptied, and the Mexican housewife who could not afford bread served packs of less nutritious instant noodles for dinner.

Impoverished Mexicans in Central Mexico and the surrounding regions depended on the corn tortilla for more than 40 percent of protein and half of daily caloric intake. In the early 1950s in the barrio of San José on the edge of Mexico City, "Esperanza filled the clay pot and set the cinnamon tea to boil. Over a hundred tortillas had to be made—twenty five each for Pedro and for Felipe, Martin, and Ricardo, the three oldest sons who worked in the fields, and ten more for Pedro's dog," noted anthropologist Oscar Lewis. Mexico needed to keep everyone eating tortillas.

The Green Revolution
In 1944, to increase the corn and wheat crop, the Mexican government had invested in a cooperative agricultural research program with the Rockefeller Foundation led by U.S. agronomist Norman Borlaug. On a global quest to "feed the hungry people of the world," Borlaug researched the best possible regional plant genetics supplemented with fertilizers and modern farming practices. Borlaug began his research project, part of the program dubbed the Green Revolution, in the northern state of Sonora where the wheat farmers thrived until stem and stripe rust devastated their crops. Borlaug bred semi-dwarf, high-yield, disease-resistant wheat varieties adapted to diverse areas of Mexico. The Sonorans, unencumbered by entrenched ways of farming, switched to the new seeds and techniques, and twenty years later exported excess wheat—after the Norteño set aside enough of the crop for the local flour tortillas.

The indigenous corn farmers in Central Mexico were a bit more resistant to change, cultivating carefully saved varieties of corn seeds on small rain-fed individual plots of communal *ejidos* established during the agrarian reform after the Mexican Revolution. A lot of corn was crucial to the traditional tortilla and the government abandoned its support of the small-scale farmers. Instead, the aggressive agribusiness producer, removed from ties to the traditions and cultural practices of ancient Mesoamerica, cultivated specific high-yield corn hybrids and accessed large tracts of farmland, credit, subsidies, and technology.

The Political Tortilla

Spurred by the politically and economically sensitive tortilla, by 1950 the Mexican government entered the tortilla business with the state-supported nixtamalized corn flour plant Maíz Industrializado SA, now known as the privately owned Minsa. Financed by the national development bank, Minsa milled subsidized corn purchased by the State Food Agency in bulk from large corn producers, and working with the Agency sold corn flour to the low-income public, mostly in agency stores.

For a time there were two viable commercial corn flour companies in Mexico, Minsa and Maseca, competing for the Mexican customer. In an effort to keep tortilla prices low and stable, the government controlled the national corn harvest and limited the amount and quality of corn available to the small neighborhood tortillerías making tortillas from masa, the traditional fresh corn dough. They sent a clear message to the Mexicans: buy corn flour, not fresh masa tortillas. The food politicians approved. Nixtamalized corn flour was convenient, saved time and labor, and remained fresh while stored in warehouses. Tortillas made from instant corn flour kept the people fed and earned votes.

GUEST ESSAY

• • • • •

The Political Significance of the Tortilla in Mexico

TONY PAYAN, UNIVERSITY OF TEXAS AT EL PASO

Food staples, daily diet components that provide much of the nutrition and energy for a person, are necessarily political. Nowhere is this truer than the humble tortilla in Mexico, where the corn flatbread is charged with cultural, historical, social, and political significance. One of the manifestations of the political significance of the tortilla, which dates back to the Aztecs and the Mayas, is its price. Mexicans are deeply sensitive to even the smallest change in the price of tortillas. In 2006 and 2007, due to a drop in the production of corn worldwide, the price of tortillas in Mexico rose quickly. The protests, political commentary, and social pressure that followed were such that President Felipe Calderón called for a national Tortilla Price Stabilization Pact. The pact, of major political importance for the Calderón administration, called on large and small producers of tortillas, including the giants Grupo Maseca and Bimbo, to impose a ceiling on the price of tortillas. The pact drew resistance from the right, which claimed government interference with market forces, and from the left, which claimed that the pact was largely voluntary, had no teeth, and left the poor vulnerable to further increases in the price of tortillas. The federal government mobilized its law enforcement apparatus to punish market speculation on tortillas, and the government bought and released major amounts of corn into the market to reduce the price of tortillas, much in the way the United States releases its oil reserves when the price of gasoline rises too quickly. Even the Maize Industry Council, the Bank of Mexico, and other actors entered the fray linking the rise in the tortilla price to class-based movements, geographically differentiated consumption, and inflation control.

The humble tortilla proved, once more, to be a powerful political symbol in Mexico, one that can mobilize an entire nation and place a national government on the defensive.

• • • • •

What did the people whose lives revolved around the tortilla think about masa harina, the corn flour creation? Private tortilla manufacturers were delighted. Dehydrated corn flour improved the consistency of manufactured tortillas and was easily blended with other dry ingredients like preservatives. Initially, labor unions objected because machines replaced workers, but as the number of commercial flour mills increased in Mexico, so did jobs. Wet grain millers who ground nixtamalized corn into masa and tortillería entrepreneurs who made tortillas from corn dough lost customers. The mother who worked outside of the home accepted the instant tortilla as quick, easy, and versatile— the lime flavor was a little mild but the tortillas were affordable. Yet loyal consumers did not entirely forsake the fresh ground corn tortilla. They agreed with journalist Alma Guillermoprieto, who compares the industrialized corn tortilla to "rounds of grilled cardboard."

Luna's Tortillas

While Mexican government officials and entrepreneurs directed a vigorous campaign to change the eating habits of Mexico tortilla lovers to instant tortillas, across the U.S. border in Dallas, Texas, María Luna recognized a business opportunity with the traditional Mexican corn tortilla.

Sharing a long border and history with Mexico, Texas absorbed a large population of Mexican immigrants and by the 1920s there were second-generation U.S.-born Mexicans. Rich or poor, Mexicans were a visible part of the community. Americanization efforts by the Anglo Texans intensified. They segregated many schools, disdained Spanish, and in the workplace tensions were high. To preserve their culture and counter the notion of the Mexican backward peasant, Mexicans formed their own private schools and community self-help societies, *mutalitas*. To honor tradition, families celebrated Mexican Independence Day and visited the graves of family with food and gifts on the Day of the Dead. And fresh tortillas from the neighborhood tortillería comforted new immigrants and connected Texas Mexicans to their home country.

In 1923 in San Luis Potosí, Mexico, María Luna was twenty-three years old and a widow with two young children. Almost straight north was the road to Texas—a link to Laredo, San Antonio, and Dallas. Luna traveled it as far as Dallas, where she settled her family in a Mexican neighborhood and then found a job at the corner grocery store. There she noticed the women coming and going each morning to buy balls of corn dough to make tortillas for their family and friends. Thus, when a customer returned a corn grinder, Luna decided to make and sell fresh tortillas and bought the grinder. She did not know how to use it or pat the dough into perfect tortillas, but the housewives who shopped at the store were the experts. She would hire them. The women tortilla makers said yes, but their husbands said no, no women of theirs would work outside the home. So Luna brought the work to the women. She cooked and soaked the corn in mineral lime solution at her home and transported it in pails to the women in their own kitchens, who ground the corn into dough and patted it into tortillas. After one year, twenty five women made over five hundred tortillas a day, sold door-to-door until business grew, and Luna opened Luna's Tortilla Factory, today a designated City of Dallas Landmark.

The Economic Tortilla

Five generations later, Luna's Tortillas still sells the taste and fragrance of nostalgia, authentic nixtamal corn tortillas, but the times and economics have changed. Are fresh tortillas, whether made from corn dough (masa), dehydrated corn flour, or wheat flour, a luxury? Does price matter for the freshest, most delicious tortilla? Compared to manufactured tortillas, fresh tortillas are expensive to buy and time consuming to prepare for the socio-economic groups who depend on tortillas three times a day and for the locals who live in the suburbs too distant from the neighborhood tortillería. For the typical restaurant owners who want convenience and profit, the made-from-scratch tortillas are impractical. For the independent tortilla maker, small scale tortillerías require start-up funds for investment and the proper technology.

The standardized manufactured tortilla, corn or wheat flour, is arguably no substitute for the "perfect" Mesoamerican tortilla, but it is healthy, contains protein, some fat, fiber and vitamins, minerals and carbohydrates, and has a mild flavor. Early tortilla production was an inefficient process that involved crude machines and challenging working conditions. Sixty years ago in Albuquerque, New Mexico, the tortilla makers at Bueno

(above left) Rolling wheat flour tortillas by hand on piecrust roller, circa 1960s, Bueno Foods. (Courtesy of Bueno Foods, Albuquerque, New Mexico)

(above right) Modern factory production of wheat flour tortillas, Rudy's Tortillas. (Courtesy of Rudy's Tortillas, Dallas, Texas)

Foods, still owned by the Baca family, rolled wheat flour tortillas by hand on a piecrust roller, a technique the founding Baca brothers borrowed from the family bakery business. Bueno Foods became the first company to commercially produce tortillas in New Mexico.

The advanced technology of tortilla equipment revolutionized the industry. The manufacturing process became cleaner and safer, and quality control improved. Production doubled, then tripled, and produced an affordable tortilla. As the market expanded, demand increased and the expanding tortilla manufacturing spawned a powerful industry. In 2013 in Dallas, Texas, Rudy's Tortillas processed approximately a million pounds of fresh corn and three hundred thousand pounds of wheat flour each week to provide tortillas for Mexican restaurants.

Big and Small Empires

Volume tortilla producers gained a business advantage of connections—loans, permits, affiliations between companies, and access to markets. At stake was a huge growth industry transformed by technology, trade, and migration. The "Tortilla King" Roberto González Barrera incurred admiration and praise, jealousy and scrutiny. Did he build his tortilla empire on favoritism?

"The relationship between Maseca and the Government, and the flash fortune it created, is a textbook case of how that system has worked," wrote journalist Anthony DePalma in the *New York Times* in 1996. "Since President Salinas's term in office began, Maseca has benefited enormously from Government policies aimed at nothing less than changing the way Mexicans eat, substituting corn flour mass-produced by Maseca for the fresh corn dough that had been the staple for generations."

Gruma, the parent company of Maseca, promptly rebutted this perception. "The company's success is due to its technological innovations in the production of tortillas . . . and is not, as your article suggests, a result of favoritism by a single political Mexican administration that followed the company's founding by 40 years," argued Eduardo Livas Jr., Chief Executive Officer of Gruma.

Some small tortilla producers took on the "Tortilla King." Particularly in Texas and California where Mission Foods dominated the market, tortilla makers filed antitrust lawsuits accusing Gruma of forcing small, competing producers out of the marketplace. According to one lawsuit reported in the *Los Angeles Times*, Gruma paid specific grocery stores "to exclude placement of competitors' tortilla products on supermarkets' shelves." The lawsuits were dismissed.

In Los Angeles in 1996, truck drivers struck Mission Guerrero, a division of Gruma's Mission Foods, and won. "My children are always asking for things I can't give them . . . meanwhile I'm working 12 or 15 hours a day, six days a week," said Ramon Alvarez in an interview with photojournalist David Bacon. After seven weeks of strike lines and stopping traffic, the tortilla-truck drivers backed by Teamsters Local 63 signed a contract with Mission Foods giving them a 22 percent overall pay increase for the life of the contract. "We can all see that the stakes are very high in this strike for the strikers themselves—and for the right of all immigrant workers to organize and live a decent life," argues Joel Ochoa, organizing director of the Los Angeles Manufacturing Project, which supported the strike.

Small empires bump up against big empires and do survive. In Mexico and the immigrant neighborhoods of the United States, for example, tortilla lovers who prefer the alkaline flavor of fresh nixtamalized corn tortillas follow their stomachs to the traditional tortillerías. In LaBelle, Florida, a citrus-growing town in an oak hammock on the shores of the tidal Caloosahatchee River, they find their way on a side street to Las Gemelas Tortilleria. "*La mezcla perfecta* (the perfect mix), made the same way my mother, my grandmother, all the way back, made tortillas," says owner Rodolfo Gamez.

Born in Michoacán, Mexico, Rodolfo Gamez immigrated to the United States when he was nine years old. His father, a migrant farm worker, preceded the family, and once his wife and children joined him, they moved from state to state, Pennsylvania to California, with the seasonal crops. "We never stayed long enough for me to finish sixth grade," Gamez says. By day the family picked apples; at night, they camped on the edge of the orchard where his mother made a fire from orchard wood and cooked store-bought corn tortillas. "No time to make her own. The tortillas burst into fire—what were they made from, paper? They tasted awful."

"But I haven't worked as hard as my father," says Gamez. "I didn't stay a field hand forever. They promoted me up to truck driver." Fifteen years ago he bought a convenience store stocked with the usual inventory yet individualized for the Mexican immigrant. *Tuna*, the fruit of the prickly pear cactus. Ropes of dried hot chiles. Cowboy boots from Michoacán. A walk-up taco stand. But Gamez was not satisfied with the tortillas. At home he ate corn tortillas made fresh by his wife and cooked on the

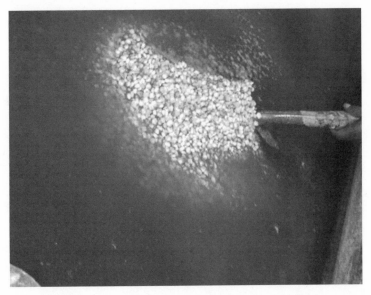

Nixtamal-steeped corn in factory vat, *Las Gemelas Tortilleria*, LaBelle, Florida.

comal brought from Mexico. In the store he sold corn flour tortillas, packaged and preserved with additives. "Only similarity
between the 'other' tortillas and tortillas made the old Mexican
way, they both were round," he says.

Gamez traveled home to Michoacán to apprentice at a tortillería and returned to Florida to open a tortilla factory down
the road from his store. He produces fresh tortillas: limited
batches of wheat flour tortillas for burritos for the farm workers,
and lots of corn tortillas, his customers' favorite. He prepares the
corn tortillas from nixtamalized corn dough, following a ninety-
year-old masa recipe learned when he was in Michoacán. "But
it is not only the recipe, it is how you make it. . . . the process
makes the difference," he says.

The process was the mechanical corn grinder rotating corn
on the basalt grinding stone, the flavor of the ancient volcanic
rock metate. The process was precise timing to cook and steep

Basalt grinding stone
for factory production of
nixtamal corn tortillas,
Las Gemelas Tortilleria,
LaBelle, Florida.

the corn in lime solution—not too long, not too short. "Like knowing how long to let good wine sit," says Gamez. The product was the perfect tortilla cooked quickly, hot off the conveyor belt, puffy with some moisture so it stayed moist when reheated at home.

When Gamez purchases corn on the international market, he competes in price for food corn with fuel ethanol corn. The more corn diverted from the grain market to make ethanol, an alternative fuel especially promoted in the United States, the higher the price for corn to make tortillas. He pays the premium price for a hybrid variety of Pioneer white dent corn specific for the nixtamal process from Rovey Seed Company in Illinois. There the corn is bagged in plastic totes the size of hay bales, loaded on a freight truck, and trucked to LaBelle. At the factory, one of the ten shift employees unloads the totes by forklift or manpower to the storage area. When they are ready to use the corn, once more they manually move the totes, this time to the factory floor, open the bags, and transfer the corn into production.

When tortilla conglomerates such as Gruma, the leader in worldwide tortilla production, and Tyson Foods, the second largest tortilla manufacturer in the United States, purchase corn and wheat, they negotiate for a volume discount, contract guaranteed prices by buying grain futures, and link with giant U.S. agricultural commodity brokers such as Archer-Daniels-Midland (ADM). At the tortilla factory, trucks and freight trains unload the corn and wheat ground into flour at the company's separate mills into the storage silos through pneumatic connections. Automated equipment and computers control the handling of the grain.

When Gamez delivers tortilla orders he travels within approximately a hundred-mile radius to local restaurants and stores. He depends on his reputation for repeat customers willing to pay a slight premium price for his tortillas, or he matches the price of the Mission Food type competition. "I can't make it in business if Mexicans won't buy my tortillas," he says.

The large-scale producers ship by tractor trailer trucks at favorable freight rates directly from their production facility to grocery store warehouses and restaurant chains. With national and international marketing their aggressive advertising costs are spread over the large volume of the company's manufactured tortilla products.

As it happened, wherever tortillas were sold—in Mexico, the United States, and internationally—the industrialization of the tortilla did not cause the traditional tortilla and its tortilla culture to disappear. In fact, the mass-produced tortilla has spread the word about the incomparable tortilla and guaranteed the tortilla's survival in the modern world.

• • • THE IMMIGRANT TORTILLA

UNDOCUMENTED

Alone,
Facing foreign lights
He hears whispered voices, distantly:
This bridge takes you to oblivion,
It changes your name.

Nothing will be yours now,
Listen to the departing train,
The wind rubbing against the evening,
Nothing will be yours now
And when you return
You'll bring under your fingernails, your touch, your
breath,
The feeling of having visited
The underside of your dreams.
Nothing will be yours now
As were the games of childhood,
Those village gardens,
The same memory.

ENRIQUE CORTÁZAR (2004)
(Translated by Jimmy Santiago Baca)

In 1994 the single strand of cable marking the international border
between San Diego, California, and Tijuana, Mexico, was replaced

with an eighteen-foot barrier. Called Operation Gatekeeper, the new border strategy by the United States began with the construction of fourteen miles of steel fence stretching from the inland desert to the beach. When construction workers reached the Pacific Ocean they kept going and sunk steel pillars into the sand three hundred feet into the ocean surf.

Supporters called it the "Fence," intended to deter unauthorized immigration and contraband and enhance national security. Opponents called it the "Border Wall," a new form of the old Berlin Wall separating East Germany from West Germany. They argued it created social divisions, encouraged migrant smuggling, and forced the desperate to seek alternative routes through the rocky canyons and dangerous desert. But the name that stuck was the "Tortilla Wall."

The farmer pushed out from worn-out land in Oaxaca; the teacher pulled to a job in Los Angeles; the Tijuana maid hired to cook and clean for the California housewife; the college student born in the United States, raised in Mexico, and living his dream; the narco-orphan child; and the people smuggler—documented and undocumented, they all began their journey with a knapsack stuffed with tortillas. To those on the American side, the "Tortilla Wall" was a symbol of complicated immigration and border security issues, separate from the tortilla cuisine consumed with gusto. For many Mexicans and Central Americans, nicknaming it the "Tortilla Wall" was an unfriendly gesture, a derogatory reference to the cultural and culinary staple created from cooking techniques dating back to Mesoamerica.

Today, almost seven hundred miles of strategically placed single, double, or triple "Tortilla Walls" stretch along the more than two thousand miles of the U.S. border with Mexico. Do the high-tech border fences reduce illegal crossings? "The fencing is just another tool that we have. It helps to slow down the entry of these people to give our agents a chance to make an arrest. Because a fence alone isn't going to stop people from coming

"Tortilla Wall" border fence looking from Las Playas in Tijuana on the Mexican side into the United States in San Diego County, California. (Courtesy of Kimberly Heinle, Trans-Border Institute, University of San Diego, San Diego, California)

in," said Supervisory Border Patrol Agent Michael Jimenez in an interview with Ruxandra Guidi. "Human beings have more ideas than any device," said an immigrant-smuggling *coyote* in the documentary The Fence.

Whether you believe the border fences are part of what needs to be reformed or part of the solution, whether you want to cut the flow of immigrants to the United States or increase the flow of ideas and services across the border, the United States and Mexico are connected. Tens of thousands of documented and undocumented immigrants, largely from Mexico and Central America, cross the Mexican border into the United States each year. For decades, waves of immigrants born in Mexico—an estimated twelve million, more than any other single country— migrated to the United States. But in 2012, the weak U.S. economy slowed jobs in the housing construction market, historically a job source for immigrant labor, while in Mexico the government broadened its free market economy. In the United States, Immigration and Custom Enforcement (ICE) agents rounded up deportations and it was harder to cross the border. The Mexican immigration wave subsided.

Still, in 2012 the Pew Hispanic Center reported that among the 50.7 million Hispanics in the United States, nearly two-thirds self-identified as being of Mexican origin. They swayed elections—71 percent of Hispanic population voted for President Obama in the 2012 election. They bought homes in the cities and rural areas. They raised their children in the United States. And Hispanics brought the tortilla to the table of even the most suspicious American nativist, ambivalent about the newcomers, yet extolling the culture in the tortilla's various forms of tacos, enchiladas, flautas, gorditas, sopaipillas, quesadillas, and burritos.

The Children of the Immigrants

For José Rubio Jr. and his family, making and selling tortillas provided an opportunity to enter the cultural and economic mainstream of middle-class America. They identified with the tortilla as an important part of their heritage and built their business around the tortilla as a marketable product.

"I was made in the U.S., but born in Mexico," says José Rubio Jr. In 1972 his father, who was traveling with his nineteen-year-old wife, had finished picking apples in the late summer in Oregon. But before he moved on to the winter crops in California, they returned home to the family homestead in rural Michoacán, where Rubio's mother, a proud Mexican, wanted her child born. Still, the opportunity for la vida mejor, the better life, was in the United States, and a year later the family left behind their Mexican roots for the other side of the border, the "pure allure of the American dream."

For Rubio's father, the path to the American dream was through tortillas. He settled his family in Mascotte, Florida, a town among the watermelon fields and citrus groves of Lake County. By day, he worked in a laundromat; in the evening he sold fresh corn tortillas door-to-door to the small but growing Mexican community.

Tortillas connected his father's customers to their culture, but for José Rubio Jr. the tortilla said he was the only Mexican in his fourth grade class. So when his teacher asked the children to describe what they had for dinner, Rubio invented a dinner of spaghetti, mashed potatoes, and macaroni and cheese—all in one meal.

Times changed. Today, more than 40 percent of Mascotte's residents are of Hispanic heritage. Downtown, a Mexican botánica sells potions and herbs and Mexican restaurants specialize in regional foods. On the outskirts is the first of two Rubio's Mexican Food Stores, the second one in nearby Leesburg. This is where the Mexicans shop for piñatas, soccer shirts, imported tamarind-flavored soda, the fruit of prickly pear cactus, and all the ingredients to prepare an authentic Mexican meal.

In the morning the Mexican women pat the corn dough into shape for corn tortillas and mix wheat flour with lard and water for flour tortillas. They cook them on the griddle, and customers line up for tacos and burritos from the in-store taqueria. At the meat counter, the butcher cuts up locally grown beef and pork and sets out jars of pork rinds and chicken feet. But Rubio's is more than a Hispanic market; it is where the newly arrived and the settled gather for a sense of the familiar in the midst of central Florida.

Far from the citrus groves of Florida, in New York City the masa-deprived who wanted the best traditional tortillas searched for a tortillería that used fresh lime-processed ground corn dough—until first-generation Mexican-American Fernando Ruiz, a New York City firefighter, and Shauna Page, with Native American roots in California, founded a destination place for authentic Mexican tortillas in Corona, a few subway stops from Manhattan.

Fernando Ruiz and Shauna Page installed machinery from Mexico, ordered non-genetically modified and nontransgenic white dent corn, listened to the advice of Ruiz's uncle, Pancho Manitas from Veracruz, Mexico, and in 2008 opened Tortilleria Nixtamal, the nixtamal tortillería making masa and fresh tortillas. "The purpose of the tortilla is to enhance the flavor of the food, not merely to hold it together," says Ruiz.

Tortilleria Nixtamal works well as a local business because freshness and authenticity are important to their customer's concept of good corn tortillas—made from masa with no preservatives, wrapped in paper, not plastic, and stored in a warming oven, never cooled. Customers come from nearby Roosevelt Avenue, the local Mexican district. Also, non-Mexicans show up, the foodies attracted by favorable reviews by New York City food editors who are willing to pay extra and travel out of their way to Queens Borough for an adventure in the preparation and consumption of distinctive nixtamal tortillas.

In 1945 it was a different world from today's foodie revolution in Dallas, Texas, when José Guerra founded the Texas Tortillas Factory. World War II ended and Texas needed workers. Under the Bracero Program alone, approximately 117,000 Mexicans left home for good-paying temporary jobs on farms in Texas.

Guerra was born in Texas, raised in San Luis Potosí, Mexico, and migrated back to Texas. At age forty-five he opened a mom-and-pop tortilla shop, his "retirement" business, in one of Dallas's bustling immigrant neighborhoods, a logical choice for the Mexican-owned tortillería catering to customers who did not venture far from their home territory.

"Start something and make something better out of it," Guerra said. He started with the comal system, producing tortillas made with the dough of lime-soaked and ground corn, cooked on the hot griddle and turned over by hand with a spatula. Three

Tortilleria Nixtamal,
Corona, New York.

generations later, Rudy's Tortillas now produces over fifteen million corn and wheat flour tortillas daily in its state-of-the-art tortilla manufacturing plant and competes on a national scale. Tortillas move down rows and rows of production lines, eventually dropping onto conveyor belts that feed them through the ovens onto the cooling belt. In 2013 Rudy's moved to a larger facility to accommodate growth. "Our passion for tortillas runs deep and is still burning strong, 68 years long and three generations and counting," says CEO Louis Guerra, grandson of founder José Guerra, who operates the company with brothers Rudy Jr. and Joe.

"We gave up the retail store when it was no longer special," says Louis Guerra. Similar to the bread industry as it matured, small regional tortilla shops gave way to consolidated, giant tortilla corporations. In the supermarket, customers selected pre-packaged, mass-produced tortillas, competitively priced and convenient. Rudy's looked for an edge in the marketplace.

Rudy's found its niche with restaurant goers, for eating habits had evolved and the tortilla had crossed cultures among diverse ethnic groups who wanted the familiar and the novel tortilla— flavor blends, organic, low-carbohydrate, and wheat flour wraps. Rudy's adapted. It changed its production and marketing plans to sell wholesale for restaurants through national food distributors, and the business hit its stride.

The Tortilla Boom

While the entrepreneurs focused on tortillas, in Piedras Negras, Mexico, across the Rio Grande from Eagle Pass, Texas, Ignacio "Nacho" Anaya, maître d' at the Victory Club, assembled the first nacho appetizer. In 1943 a group of officers' wives from Fort Duncan Air Base in Eagle Pass crossed the border to shop and stopped by the club restaurant operated by Rodolfo de Los Santos for a late-afternoon Mexican snack. But the cook had gone home for the day. "Let me go quick and fix something for you," Ignacio Anaya Jr. recalled his father told the women. In the kitchen Ignacio grated yellow Wisconsin cheese over a pile of homemade tostadas, the fried corn tortilla chips cut into triangles, and placed them under the broiler. He topped the concoction with sliced jalapeno and served it on a large platter, paired with frosty margaritas. Reportedly, Mamie Finan, one of the satisfied customers, named the snack "Nacho's Especiales," said Ignacio Anaya Jr. Aficionados shortened to it to just "nachos."

Yet not everyone in the business of making tortillas traces their heritage back to Mesoamerica. It was the 1950s in California, and Glen Bell sold quickly prepared hamburgers at Bell's Burgers, competing with a lot of other entrepreneurs, including the McDonald brothers. At the time, locals accustomed to Cal-Mex food in California or Tex-Mex in Texas varied their hamburger diet with the taco, the small, soft, corn or wheat flour tortilla folded around meat or beans and chile. The taco was

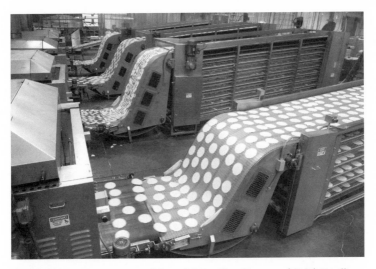

Manufactured tortillas on conveyor belt, Rudy's Tortillas. (Courtesy of Rudy's Tortillas, Dallas, Texas)

High-technology tortilla factory production area, Rudy's Tortillas. (Courtesy of Rudy's Tortillas, Dallas, Texas)

largely unknown in other parts of the United States—a gap Bell filled with Taco Tia, El Taco, and in 1962 his signature Taco Bell.

"We changed the eating habits of an entire nation," claimed Bell in *Taco Titan: The Glen Bell Story*. In the process he also changed the corn tortilla to conform to Taco Bell's fast food version of the taco shell—a pre-fried, crunchy-hard tortilla wrapped in plastic until ready to fill in an instant with beef or chicken, heat, and serve.

Taco Bell spread its definition of Mexican fare from coast to coast. "It may not be authentic and it may not be gourmet but Taco Bell helped familiarize Americans with Mexicans and their culture," says journalist Gustavo Arellano. Yet when Taco Bell attempted to take the taco to the homeland of the tortilla it baffled Mexicans. "It's like bringing ice to the Arctic," said Mexican historian Carlos Monsiváis. In less than eighteen years Taco Bell failed twice south of the border. In 1992 in Mexico City, and then in 2007 in the northern state of Monterrey, Taco Bell opened restaurants branded "Taco Bell Is Something Else"—an American fast food alternative that did not pretend to be authentic Mexican. The doors closed in 2010.

Elsewhere, Chipotle Mexican Grill, founded by Steve Ells in 1993 in Colorado and one of the largest Mexican food chains in the United States, defined the burrito with its own twist on the ingredients wrapped in a wheat flour tortilla. Ells promised "food with integrity"—nutritious, fresh, and economical. The Americanized burrito was different from the stuffed tortilla served at the lunchtime food stalls in Mexico, but the concept was the same: cheap fast food. The market for Mexican food grew, trade expanded, and food tastes diversified. American or Mexican, tortilla fans decided that cheap and fast could also be good burritos.

No one knows the exact origin of the word "burrito" but it comes from a term for a small donkey, or in Spanish, a little *burro*. In the depths of the copper and silver mines in colonial Sonora, Mexico, the miners sat on the ground beside the burros used

Mexican burro, early 1900s. (Courtesy of El Paso County Historical Society, El Paso, Texas)

as pack animals and ate stuffed flour tortillas, the tortilla of the northern Mexican frontier. The story goes that they named their portable lunch "burrito" for their lunch mate, the burro. However, on the open range of the frontier the early Hispanic cowboy (vaquero) claimed the name. He carried flour tortillas filled with beans, called *tacos de frijoles*, in his saddlebags laid across the back of his horse. The tortillas in the saddlebags were as close a companion as the traditional sidekick of the horse, the burro. Thus, the burrito. The burrito again showed up in the 1940s at the U.S.-Mexico border in Ciudad Juárez, Mexico, when the customers of Los Burritos said they were "going to the burritos" to buy the well-known filled tortillas. By then the burrito had migrated away from the Mexico and Southwest border and was on its way to become as much a part of the American food culture as the hamburger.

Tortilla in the Lab

Without the tortilla there would be no taco or burrito or nachos. Why improve the popular tortilla? As wholesome as the tortillas prepared from lime-soaked corn are, the corn tortilla is even more nutritious when fortified with essential vitamins and minerals, most important for the families of Central America and Mexico who still depend on the corn tortilla as the dominant staple food.

In the United States the tortilla is a mainstream food and part of a varied diet. There is plenty of poverty and poor nutrition in the United States, but the standard breakfast cereal, bread, and products made from wheat flour all are fortified with micronutrients that support growth and protect against disease. In Mexico and Central America the very poor eat corn tortillas three times a day, often without supplementation from other high-quality foods. These are the people that tortilla-fortification programs help.

The corn tortilla can be made from dehydrated corn flour, masa harina, or corn dough, masa. In Mexico, Sergio Serna-Saldivar at Tecnológico de Monterrey led the corn flour fortification program. In the United States, food scientist Michael Dunn and his research team at Brigham Young University led the wet-ground nixtamal corn dough fortification project.

When Michael Dunn began the three-year project in 2004 on how to fortify corn dough tortillas in Mexico, 60 percent of the people in Mexico consumed corn tortillas prepared from fresh nixtamal (the lime-steeped corn kernels) instead of dehydrated corn flour. The challenge was to produce commercially available fortified tortillas directly from fresh ground masa to reach the large segment of the Mexican population that was not consuming tortillas made from fortified flour.

The research, funded by SUSTAIN, a U.S.-based nonprofit organization, required patience and persistence. For the consumer, the appearance, color, texture, and flavor of the traditional tortilla had to be preserved. When the researchers added ferrous sulfate, the tortilla turned greenish; when they added another source of iron, it cast a reddish-brown tint, unacceptable to Mexicans accustomed to white tortillas. They experimented

Tortilla former at small neighborhood mill, Mexico, 2005. The ball of freshly ground corn dough (masa) on the top feeds into the sheeter/cutter. The tortillas drop onto a conveyor belt that takes them through the oven. (Courtesy of Michael Dunn)

with nine different iron sources until they found one that did not affect the color or flavor.

For the small-scale entrepreneur millers, the specialized equipment had to be an affordable investment. Dunn contacted one equipment manufacturer who considered tortillas "perfect as they were, almost sacred," but another Mexican manufacturer was intrigued with the project and adapted the technology for the mills at an affordable price. As a result of the fortification process, the corn tortillas supplied nearly three times as much thiamin, niacin, and zinc; four times as much iron and riboflavin; and five times the folic acid compared to regular tortillas. Dunn, who previously did product development for Häagen-Dazs, admits it was exciting to develop a new ice cream flavor and then see a pint or quart of the finished product in the supermarket. Yet, when he sees children at the neighborhood mills in Mexico buying fortified tortillas he realizes these tortillas are "much more worthwhile to them than a pint of Häagen-Dazs is to your average consumer."

Change and Continuity

Even with technology to adapt the ancient Mesoamerican formulas to modern tortilla preparation and tastes, change represents a challenge for continuity of traditions. "Neza," an anthropology graduate student in Postclassical Mexico at Tulane University in New Orleans, Louisiana, asserted his cultural identity by changing his name.

His full name is Nezahualcoyotl Xiuhtecutli—the name of a king, Nezahualcóyotl, the philosopher tlatoani of the Aztec city-state of Texcoco, and the fire deity, Xiuhtecutli, often referred to the "Old God," the fire in the hearth of a home. Neza, easier to pronounce than Nezahualcoyotl, was born Aquiles Martínez in Mexico City. When he was fourteen years old, his family immigrated to North Carolina. When he was twenty-seven years old, he changed his name.

"Of course, the tortilla has always been a component of my identity," he says. At home, his mother cooked Mexican-style corn tortillas for his father from Veracruz, Mexico, and wheat flour tortillas, a reflection of her Chihuahua roots in northern Mexico. Yet the tortilla was more than food, la tradición mexicana, a visit home in the kitchen of the immigrant family. The tortilla tradition was a bridge to Mexican culture . . . the offerings for the return of the souls of the dead on the Day of the Dead; the warm comal hearth, the heart of the pre-Hispanic home; the art of Tortilla Makers and The Grinder, depicted by Diego Rivera. All of this honored Neza's Mesoamerican heritage. From now on, Neza said, he would be known by his classical Nahuatl name, the language of the Aztec. The tortilla comes full circle from pre-conquest Mesoamerica to the present day.

Face of Jesus on Tor-
tilla. (Courtesy of
Tom Wilbur)

The Global Tortilla

This is the time of the global tortilla. It connects people and
introduces the tortilla culture from the ancient past to contemporary society. It inspires the technology to make special corn
tortillas that look and taste similar to Motecuhzoma's tlaxcalli
and improve children's lives one meal at a time. Asians eat wheat
tortilla spring rolls in China. Americans consume more corn and
flour tortillas than bagels, and 2011 sales were more than $8 bil-
lion. The Brits perceive the wheat flour tortilla wrap, filled with
the familiar cheese, canned tuna, ham, or chicken, as a healthy
alternative to white sandwich bread, and 2010 sales increased
17 percent. Astronauts cook burritos in space because, "you can
do so much with a tortilla," says astronaut Sandra Magnus. A
housewife in New Mexico sees the image of the face of Jesus
Christ on the "Miracle Tortilla." What does the international success of the tortilla tell us?

On the culinary battlefield, the mass-produced tortilla battles
with the "real" tortilla made to order in front of your eyes. The
point is "how the culture and plants and foods come together,"
says renowned Mexican cook and author Diana Kennedy.
Defenders of the food tradition believe the tortilla is all about the
stretched flour tortilla made from landrace white Sonora wheat,

one of the oldest surviving wheat varieties of northern Mexico, and the corn tortilla made from lime-soaked native corn ground into masa on the metate. Restaurant chains and corporate manufacturers challenge the tradition with changes in the production and marketing to spread the tortilla around the globe. In the world of the global tortilla, you can sample both.

GUEST ESSAY
· · · · ·
The Importance of the Tortilla in Oaxaca

PILAR CABRERA, CHEF, RESTAURANTE LA OLLA, OAXACA DE JUÁREZ

I am Pilar Cabrera, a chef with a passion for the food of my homeland, Oaxaca, Mexico. I have lived in my city, Oaxaca de Juárez, for over 40 years. For a short time I lived in Mexico City, and what I missed the most were the tortillas made by my grandmother.

In every town in Oaxaca, the tortilla is our basic food staple. Hard or soft, big or small, the tortilla is indispensable for breakfast, at our main meal (*comida*), and the light evening meal (*cena*). And there is nothing better than to eat a freshly made tortilla! In this part of the world, instead of accompanying meals with bread we use the tortilla, and in some communities the tortilla takes the place of the spoon.

In Oaxaca there are vestiges of the first native local corn species, and that is why there is such a variety. Add to this the favorable climate and our fertile soil and you understand we find a great diversity of corn sold in the markets of the adjacent towns.

At this time the problems I encounter are:

· Farmers increasingly emigrate and leave their lands and corn crops. Thus, it's difficult to find the variety of native corn in the local markets.

· The *tortilleras* (tortilla makers) are quitting tortilla making, because they prefer to work easier jobs than making tortillas eight hours a day for low pay.

· The quality of the tortillas we are finding in the markets is no longer the same, because many tortilleras combine their corn masa with Maseca tortilla flour.

· Since the store-made tortillas are the cheapest, lower-income families buy tortillas in the tortilla stores. These tortillas are found even at the festivities of some towns. As for the cost of the tortillas made by hand and the machine-made ones, there is a great difference. There are restaurants where now they only serve machine-made tortillas.

For my family and me, the base of our sustenance is the tortilla; fresh and recently made. I list a few names we use here for the different types of tortillas. *Memelas* are thick tortillas, which we almost always serve with beans and cheese. *Blandas* are indispensable on our table at lunch time. *Tlayudas* can only be found in Oaxaca—these we can eat by themselves or as a main dish: eaten for breakfast, prepared with black bean puree, unrefined pork lard, and cheese, served open or closed. There are *totopos, tostadas,* and more.

We must teach the new generations everything involving the topic of corn and protect it, because one day it might run out, and then we will not be able to enjoy our tortillas. All of us who eat good tortillas are the ones who by consuming them are contributing to the economy of the families who produce them. In this way the tortilla-making tradition will not be lost. My children are learning this from me, and they have learned the taste of a good tortilla.

· · · · ·

There are compromises. Instead of walking to the neighborhood mill in her hometown of Ixmiquilpan, Mexico, for sacks of fresh ground masa, Mercedes Secundino pats tortillas made from dehydrated nixtamalized corn flour mix, but adds no preservatives or dough conditioners, and cooks two or three at a time on the griddle for her Hispanic customers at La Media Luna in Clearwater, Florida.

In Ciudad Juárez, Mexico, cafeteria manager Miguel Ángel González supplies tortillas every day around the clock to production line workers in the maquila, short for maquiladora, a foreign-owned manufacturing facility in Mexico—corn tortillas for the newcomers from Central Mexico, and wheat flour tortillas for the Juárez natives. "Most Mexicans prefer fresh tortillas

Tacos de nopales from *Restaurante La Olla, Oaxaca, Mexico*. *(Courtesy of Pilar Cabrera)*

from the tortillería, but they buy them from grocery stores, too, to save time or when the tortillería is closed," he says.

Contemporary Hispanic women save homemade tortillas for special occasions. They live in the modern world, yet preserve a space in their life for the traditional tortilla. "The tortilla is a source of pride," says Tampa Bay's Lourdes Mayorga, who traces her heritage to the Otomí people from the region of Hidalgo, Mexico.

Yet in Mexico in recent years sales in corn tortillas have declined, while in the United States and overseas tortilla sales have increased, spurred by the popularity of packaged wheat flour tortillas available in every grocery store and trendy tortilla wraps, ready-made for takeout or prepared as a restaurant meal. In 2002 in Mexico the average daily consumption of corn tortillas per person was 548 pounds. In 2010 the daily consumption was 346 pounds, according to the Mexican National Household Income Expenditure Survey (ENIGH in Spanish). Mexicans will not stop eating tortillas, and many, particularly those who feel a strong connection between the tortilla and the ancient origins of their common ancestry, prefer corn tortillas with the strong alkaline flavor of the nixtamal process. Fewer women prepare the corn tortillas by hand, although tucked away in rural indigenous communities, such as the Otomí along the Laja River in Guanajuato, the women, young and old, commonly make tortillas by hand to preserve their tradition and identity. But since the elimination of price controls in the late 1990s and the increase in the price of corn, the corn tortilla, produced manually or by machine, is no longer the cheap staple. And today the growing middle-class has greater prosperity and choices. Tortillas, viewed by some as the food of the poor, compete with Mexican-infused versions of subs, pizza, and hamburgers.

The Modern with the Traditional

There are the regional traditional tortillas outside Mexico in countries like Nicaragua. "I have eaten and absolutely love *güirilas*. They are made with new corn, so they are a seasonal treat. They have a rich, very unique, and sweet taste. We used to eat them with *cuajada*, a type of soft, salty cheese, when visiting the countryside or the cool mountain towns," says Nicaraguan-born Ramses Omar Cabrales. Though the Mesoamerican corn tortilla, named by the Spanish, did not make it to Spain. At the time of the conquest, the Spaniards transported a steady stream of New World products across the ocean, but the traditional tortilla stayed behind—only a skilled and patient tortilla maker could make nixtamal corn dough and pat it into tortillas. In Spain, the Spanish tortilla is a Spanish omelet made of eggs and potatoes and fried in olive oil.

Beyond Mexico, the tortilla moves from a strictly ethnic food to a mainstream food. Mix-and-match tortillas reflect the new market of healthy, flavored varieties for more and more applications of the ancient staple. Mexican poet Octavio Paz contended, "the melting pot is a social idea that, when applied to culinary art, produces abominations." True, the tortilla is no longer limited to the traditional corn or wheat flour tortilla, but consumers today like options—spinach, garlic and herb, Indian curry, low-carb, low-fat, gluten-free, red corn, blue corn, multigrain, and organic. And why not experiment? In Atlanta, Georgia, the Solis family–owned La Chiquita Tortilla offers southern-style wraps: "New! Hickory BBQ and Key Lime." The global tortilla is not static.

And while the new wave of the tortilla of *nuevo* Mexican cuisine is pricier and fancier than its forebear, it remains the Mesoamerican-inspired tortilla. "We designed the menu with the idea that most ingredients worth eating can benefit by being placed atop a well-made tortilla," says Alex Stupak, a former pastry chief who opened Empellón Taquería in New York City. In Los Angeles, Chef John Rivera Sedlar, acclaimed for his modern Southwest cuisine, creates *tortillas florales* (floral tortillas), by pressing edible flower petals (pansies, roses, nasturtiums, or squash blossoms) into nixtamalized corn dough formed into tortillas. Enrique Olvera, chef of Mexico City's Pujol, creates the "Hidden Egg," a crispy corn tortilla filled with mashed beans and the "perfect egg." And in Tucson, Arizona, Chef Janos Wilder incorporates native ingredients of the local Pima and Maricopa Indians around a hand-stretched wheat flour tortilla. "I always wait for the crops to come up. Then we start tasting and thinking," he says. Each with their distinctive cooking style innovates yet respects the tortilla tradition.

The Cross-Cultural Tortilla

The tortilla crosses cultures, a consequence of the flow of people, ideas, technology, and trade. The tortilla can bring to mind images of cheap peasant food, undocumented migrants, immigrant factory sweatshops—or it can shift awareness to the rich cultural history of the tortilla and how the tortilla has changed the way we think about traditions, industrialized food, healthy cuisine, and the people who live across borders.

What makes the tortilla so great? To celebrate the tortilla, it is important to go back in time. To tortillas for the Maya gods.

To the Mesoamerican cooks who simmered the hard kernels of corn in an alkali solution of mineral lime and created superior corn dough, nixtamal masa. To the Mexican woman on her hands and knees rolling the mano over the metate to grind corn to make fresh, warm corn tortillas. To the stubborn tortilla that persevered in spite of the Spanish conquerors who brought their gift of European bread. To northern Mexico, the land of the enormous white wheat flour tortillas. To the frontier tortilla and the Americanization of the stuffed burrito.

In the 1940s the Old El Paso Company shipped tortillas in a can to Americans who could not find a local tortilla factory. Today, tortillas—whether mass-produced, packaged, and distributed worldwide to large chain stores and restaurants, or with the resurgence of "authentic" food made fresh in a local tortillería—are everywhere.

"We always have around a package of flour tortillas, because they are so versatile . . . we eat them instead of bread, as a wrap filled with grilled chicken and salad greens, or scrambled eggs and salsa, or even hummus, instead of pita bread," says a working mother in rural New York. She admits she misses the taste of handmade fresh tortillas available when she lived in Manhattan, yet tortillas from the grocery store are convenient and easy to prepare.

"The tortilla is a delicious part of any Mexican meal, whether it is in chip or tortilla form," says fourteen-year old Allison Nastasi in Atlanta, Georgia. "It means Mom's amazing enchiladas and delicious leftovers," says her brother, Kevin. "A tortilla is Mexican to me. It is a key ingredient of what I consider Mexican food—tacos, enchiladas and quesadillas . . . all entrees to be enjoyed at least once a week with a margarita or Corona," says his father, Joe.

"When I lived in Mexico, my favorite days were when we ate handmade tortillas right off the comal," says Margarita Vargas-Betancourt, an archivist and ethnohistorian.

I was born in Mexico City in the 1970s. Back then eating tortillas meant going everyday to the tortillería to buy two kilos of tortillas. Every street had a tortillería. You brought your own piece of cloth to wrap them and a plastic bag to keep them warm. My favorite part was to grab a tortilla before the tortillera (woman who made tortillas) wrapped them. There was usually a saltshaker on the counter. You could take some salt for your tortilla and eat it on the way home. Now that I live in the U.S., I buy tortillas in the grocery store. Some are very scary; they last for months in the refrigerator and don't go bad. Others are okay, but never as good as tortillas in my childhood. Tortillas are as natural to me as speaking Spanish, and when I speak Spanish I don't think about how Indo-European languages gave way to Spanish or how this language got to the Americas.

"But what I miss about Mexico most is its food," says Vargas-Betancourt. A great tortilla is worth skipping dessert.

Notes

The notes cited here are a guide for the reader who wants to explore the cultural history of the tortilla. Full bibliographic information on the sources below is in the Selected Bibliography.

Prologue

Eva Ybarra relates her story through in-person and phone interviews. For the role of the Mexican Miracle and the bracero program, see Acuña, *Occupied America*, and MacLachlan and Beezley, *El Gran Pueblo*. For the tortilla crisis, see Ochoa, *Feeding Mexico*. Oscar Lewis described life in a Mexican village in *Tepoztlán: Village in Mexico*. For background about the history and culture of Hispanics in the United States, see Jiménez, Kanellos, and Esteva-Fabregat, *Handbook of Hispanic Cultures in the United States*.

Chapter One

The story of the contemporary Zinacantecos is taken from Vogt, *Tortillas for the Gods*. The overview of the civilizations of Mesoamerica follows Coe, *The Maya*; Coe and Koontz, *Mexico: From the Olmecs to the Aztecs*; and Carmack, Gasco, and Gossen, *The Legacy of Mesoamerica*. For a translation of the *Popul Vul*, see Tedlock. For the Aztec and Maya creation stories, see Taube, *Aztec and Maya Myths*.

The history of corn is covered in Fussell, *The Story of Corn*; Warman, *Corn & Capitalism*; and Esteva and Marielle, *Sin maíz no hay paíz*. Sophie Coe, in *America's First Cuisines*, and Pilcher, *¡Que vivan los tamales!*, discuss the Mesoamerican food legacy and the significance of the nixtamal process. See Cortés, *Letters From Mexico*, for an account of Motecuhzoma's tortilla gifts to Cortés.

For accounts of archaeological excavations, see Cheetham, "Corn, Colanders, and Cooking," and Grove, *Ancient Chalcatzingo*. Correspondence with anthropologists Frances Berdan, David Cheetham, George Cowgill, Gary Feinman, David Grove, Laura Kosakowsky, Susan Milbrath, John Staller, Barbara Stark, and agronomist Lloyd Rooney contributed to the evidence-based origin of the nixtamal process and the tortilla. See Bauer, "Millers and Grinders," for the role of the metate. The advent of the portable tortilla in Oaxaca is taken from Feinman, "The Emergence of Specialized Ceramic Production in Formative Oaxaca"; and Feinman, Blanton, and Kowalewski, "Market System Development in the Prehispanic Valley of Oaxaca, Mexico." The story of Matilda and hearth excavations in the Valley of Oaxaca is derived from correspondence with anthropologist Ronald Faulseit.

To view the tortilla art of Joe Bravo, see http://www.joebravo.net.

The recipe for corn tortillas prepared by Southwest cooks when New Mexico was part of Mexico is from Fergusson, *Mexican Cookbook*.

For a video demonstration about the preparation of nixtamal corn tortillas, see the Center for Foods of the Americas, http://www.ciaprochef.com/CFA/.

Chapter Two

The accounts of the Aztec culture follow Sahagún, *General History of the Things of New Spain*; Berdan and Anawalt, *The Essential Codex Mendoza*; Coe and Koontz, *Mexico: From the Olmecs to the Aztecs*; Carrasco, *Daily Life of the Aztecs*; and Durán, *The Aztecs*. For accounts of the Maya, see Coe, *The Maya*, and Landa, *The Maya: Diego de Landa's Account of Affairs of the Yucatan*. For Mesoamerican history, see the Foundation for the Advancement of Mesoamerican Studies (FAMSI), http://famsi.org. Sophie Coe in *America's First Cuisines* describes the culinary and cultural history of the Aztec, the Maya, and the Inca in pre-Hispanic Latin America.

The tradition of the cut-paper tortilla napkins is taken from correspondence with anthropologist Alan Sandstrom, and discussed in Sandstrom, *Corn Is in Our Blood*, and Sandstrom and Effrein Sandstrom, *Traditional Papermaking and Paper Cult Figures of Mexico*. The story of Leonel Pérez, a contemporary Maya, is derived from in-person interviews. For the story of nakara in the Mixtec culture, see Monaghan, *The Covenants with Earth and Rain*.

Chapter Three

For personal accounts of the Spanish conquest of Mesoamerica, see Cortés, *Letters From Mexico*; Díaz del Castillo, *The True History of the Conquest of New Spain*; and Landa, *The Maya*. For accounts of Mesoamerica at the time of the conquest, see Pohl, *John Pohl's Mesoamerica*; Dúran, *The Aztecs*; Gibson, *The Aztecs Under Spanish Rule*; Thomas, *Conquest*; and Coe, *The Maya*.

For the customs and economy in New Spain, see Earle, *The Body of the Conquistador*; Long-Solís, *Conquista y comida*; and Long-Solís and Vargas, *Food Culture in Mexico*. Sophie Coe gives a vivid description of the Spanish banquet in *America's First Cuisines*. For an outsider's view of life in Mexico under Spanish rule, see Calderón de la Barca, *Life in Mexico*. The role of the adapted sacrament in *Exercicio quotidiano* comes from Muñon, *Codex Chimalpahin*. The story of the Otomí ceremonial tortilla tradition is taken from Ramírez, *Tortillas Ceremoniales*, published by the Arts Center of Guanajuato, Mexico. For an overview of the enduring tortilla, see *El maíz, fundamento de la cultura popular Mexicana*, from the Museo Nacional de Culturas Populares. Alonso Ortiz Galan facilitated research at the National Council for Cultural Arts, Mexico.

Pati Jinich, http://www.patismexicantable.com, presents the mole poblano recipe.

Chapter Four

For ancient history of the Southwest, see Haury, *Prehistory of the American Southwest*, and Lekson, *A History of the Ancient Southwest*. For the account of Coronado's exploratory expedition, see Flint and Cushing Flint, *Documents of the Coronado Expedition*, and Hammond, *Coronado's Seven Cities*. The accounts of Spanish colonization follow Spicer, *Cycles of Conquest*; Hammond and Rey, *Don Juan de Oñate*; Hart, *Zuni and the Courts*; Kessell, *Spain in the Southwest*; and Kessell, *Pueblos, Spaniards, and the Kingdom of New Mexico*.

The corn culture is discussed in Beck, "Archaeological Signatures of Corn Preparation in the U.S. Southwest"; Mills, *Identity, Feasting, and the Archaeology of the Greater Southwest*; Waters, *Book of the Hopi*; and Cushing, *Zuni Breadstuff*. Correspondence with anthropologists Richard Ford, Margaret Beck, and Barbara Mills contribute to the discussion. For food gathering and preparation, see Rea, *At the Desert's Green Edge*; Nabhan, *The Desert Smells Like Rain*; and Frank, *Foods of the Southwest Indian Nations*. The case of the Sephardic families is taken from Ferry and Nathan, *Mistaken Identity?* and interviews with Rabbi Arnold Mark Belzer.

The story of Eusebio Francisca Kino is found in *Kino's Historical Memoir of Pimería Alta*, translated by Bolton; and Treutlein, *The Economic Regime of the Jesuits Missions in Eighteenth Century Sonora*. The accounts of the wheat culture in Sonora follow Pfefferkorn, *Sonora*; Miller, *Wheat Production in Europe and America*; West, *Sonora*; Yetman, *Conflict in Colonial Sonora*; Tinker-Salas, *In the Shadow of the Eagles*; and Alvarez, "And Wheat Completed the Cycle." Anthropologist Maribel Alvarez, an invaluable research resource, tells the story of the Sonora flour tortilla.

The recipe for New Mexico flour tortillas is taken from Fergusson, *Mexican Cookbook*.

Chapter Five

Lillian Trujillo, a sixth-generation resident of San Elizario, tells her story through in-person interviews and correspondence. For a description of the Salt War, see Sonnichsen, "Salt War of San Elizario." The accounts of Texas follow Alonzo, *Tejano Legacy*; Arreola, *Tejano South Texas*; and Acuña, *Occupied America*. The story of the pioneer Brown family is taken from Schlissel, Gibbens, and Hampsten, *Far From Home*. The accounts of California follow Myers, *Ho for California!*; Strehl, *Encarnación's Kitchen*; Acuña, *Occupied America*; and Pitt, *The Decline of the Californios*. Correspondence with Dan Strehl provided background information of Californio culinary history.

For a discussion of the Porfirio Díaz regime, see Pilcher, *¡Que vivan los tamales!*; Beezley, *Judas at the Jockey Club*; and MacLachlan and Beezley, *El Gran Pueblo*. The role of the soldaderas in the Mexican Revolution is covered in Salas, *Soldaderas in the Mexican Military*; MacLachlan and Beezley, *El Gran Pueblo*; and Womack, *Zapata and the Mexican Revolution*. The Public Broadcasting Service (PBS) presents *The Storm that Swept Mexico*, the story of the Mexican Revolution.

The sopaipillas recipe comes from Lillian Trujillo, courtesy of the *San Elizario Genealogy and Historical Society Cookbook*, San Elizario, Texas.

Chapter Six

The account of Hernández and conditions at the cornmill is taken from Fernández-Acevez, "Once We Were Corn Grinders." The role of the industrialized tortilla follows Gruma, *Sixty Years Gruma*; Minsa's website; Pilcher, *¡Que vivan los tamales!*; Arellano, *Taco USA*; Muñoz, *Transnational Tortillas*; and Baker, *Corn Meets Maize*. A tour of the modern Minsa cornmill provided background information. Correspondence with food scientist Michael Dunn contributed to the discussion.

For case studies about impoverished Mexicans, see Lewis, *Five Families*. For the role of Norman Borlaug and the Green Revolution, see Hesser, *The Man Who Fed the World*. The accounts of the political tortilla follow Ochoa, *Feeding Mexico*; Lind and Barham, *The Social Life of the Tortilla*. Nickerson and Dochuk, *Sunbelt Rising*; and Pilcher, *Planet Taco*. Through interviews and correspondence with Tony Payan, political scientist, the significance of the political tortilla is discussed. Payan contributes the guest essay.

Guillermoprieto's lament about the taste of the industrialized tortilla is quoted from "In Search of the Real Tortilla." The story of Luna's Tortillas is derived from an in-person interview and correspondence with Fernando Luna Jr. For the Mission Foods conflict, see DePalma, "How a Tortilla Empire Was Built on Favoritism"; Bacon, "Taking on the Tortilla King"; and Dickerson, "Small Tortilla Makers Lose Anti-Trust Suit Against Rival." The story of Las Gemelas Tortilleria is derived from in-person interviews with Rodolfo Gamez.

Chapter Seven

Enrique Cortázar, Agregado Cultural at the Consulado General de México in El Paso, Texas, composed the poem, "Undocumented." Through interviews and correspondence he contributed to the discussion about the cultural history of Mexico. For the role of the "Tortilla Wall," see the Trans-Border Institute (TBI), University of San Diego; Robbins, "San Diego Fence Provides Lessons In Border Control"; Jiménez, "Border Fence Into Pacific Ocean To Be Rebuilt"; and Kennedy, The Fence, HBO documentary.

The stories of present-day tortillerías are derived from in-person interviews with José Rubio Jr. at Rubio's Mexican Food Store; Fernando Ruiz and Shauna Page at Tortilleria Nixtamal; and Louis Guerra at Rudy's Tortillas. For the origin of the nacho, see Haram, "The History of the Nacho." For the origin of Taco Bell, see Baldwin, Taco Titan, and for Chipotle, see http://www.chipotle.com. The story of the "burrito" is taken from Arellano, Taco USA; Pilcher, Planet Taco; Castro, Chicano Folklore; and oral legends.

The accounts of nutrient-enhanced tortillas follow Serna-Saldivar, "Research Developments in the Science, Technology and Nutritional Value of Maize-Based Nixtamalized Foods"; SUSTAIN, the alliance for better food and farming; and research led by food scientists Michael Dunn, Sergio Serna-Saldivar, and agronomist Lloyd Rooney. Correspondence with Dunn and Serna-Saldivar contributed to background information.

Nezahualcoyotl Xiuhtecutli (Neza) tells his story through in-person interviews and correspondence. The importance of the present-day tortilla is derived from interviews with Mercedes and Israel Secundino at La Media Luna; Miguel Ángel González at a maquila (factory) in Ciudad Juárez, Mexico; Odilon Mezquite and Lourdes Mayorga at the Mexican Council of Tampa Bay; and José Solis at La Chiquita Tortilla. See Christie, *Kitchen Space*; and Counihan, *A Tortilla Is Like Life*, for the role of the tortilla in the everyday life. Alonso Ortiz Galan from the National Council for Culture and the Arts, Mexico, contributed to the discussion about the tortilla culture. Ramses Omar Cabrales contributed the story of güirilas in Nicaragua. In the guest essay, Chef Pilar Cabrera tells the story of the tortilla tradition in Oaxaca.

For statistics see the Pew Hispanic Center, http://www .pewhispanic.org; American Institute of Baking International, http://www.aibonline.org; Tortilla Industry of America, http:// www.tortilla-info.com; and Mexican Ministry of Economy, http://www.economia.gob.mx.

For the role of globalization, see Jayasanker, *Sameness in Diversity*; Cowen, *Is Globalization Changing the Way the World Eats*; Arellano, *Taco USA*; and Pilcher, *Planet Taco*.

Glossary

acequias: Cooperative irrigation systems used in New Spain.

atole: Gruel made from corn dough (masa); from the Nahuatl *atolli*.

bracero: Mexican laborer allowed in the United States for a limited time as a seasonal worker.

burrito: Wheat flour tortilla wrapped into a cylindrical shape to enclose a filling.

cal: Processed lime obtained by baking limestone at a high temperature to calcine it, changing the chemical composition to calcium oxide, easily ground into a powder. When combined with water, it produces slaked lime (calcium hydroxide). It can be used to make alkaline water for nixtamal corn.

champurrado: Chocolate-based drink thickened with masa, the corn dough used to make tortillas.

chinampas: Small, rectangular, raised agriculture areas of fertile swampland cultivated by the Aztec.

coa: Pre-Hispanic digging stick, typically used as a farming tool to plant corn.

comal: Heavy griddle to cook tortillas.

criollos: Mexican-born Spaniards.

crypto-Jews: "Hidden Jews," a group of Sephardic Jewish who fled from Spain to Mexico and New Mexico to escape the Inquisition.

encomienda: Spanish colonial system demanding tribute and labor from the indigenous people.

hacienda: Large Spanish estate or plantation.

hidalgo: Lowest order of Spanish nobility.

horno: Adobe brick outdoor oven, typically used to bake bread.

indigenous: Term used to describe the native peoples of North and South America.

maize: Corn (*Zea mays*); from the Spanish *maíz* and Taíno *mahiz*.

mano: Hand-held stone used to grind corn on a grinding stone.

masa: Nixtamal corn dough.

masa harina: Dehydrated corn flour.

mestizos: People of mixed Spanish and indigenous ancestry.

metate: Volcanic-rock grinding stone used to prepare nixtamal.

Mexican Miracle: Mexico's economic, educational, and industrial development strategy from the 1940s to 1970s.

molcajete: "Stone mortar" used to grind chiles and herbs.

molino de nixtamal: Nixtamal cornmill.

mulattos: Part European and African.

nakara: Strong collective bond between family, community, and the Mixtec culture in Oaxaca, Mexico.

nixtamalization: Process whereby corn is cooked in a mineral lime water solution to loosen the hard endosperm that protects the corn kernel and increase the nutritional value released from the corn kernels. The alkaline corn is ground into dough, masa, to make tortillas.

nopal: Member of the *Opuntia* cacti family, commonly called "prickly pear."

Norteño: Person from northern Mexico.

piki bread: Bread made from blue cornmeal and baked in thin sheets by the Southwest Indians.

posolli: Maya corn drink.

repartimiento: Colonial forced labor system imposed upon the indigenous population of Spanish America.

soldaderas: Female camp followers, companions, and "fighters" who made an important contribution to both the federal and rebel armies of the Mexican Revolution.

tlatoani: Nahuatl term for supreme ruler, "he who speaks."

tlaxacalli: Nahuatl name for tortilla.

torteadora or tortillera: Woman who makes tortillas in tortillería.

tortilla: Spanish term for a little cake (torta), the thin unleavened Mesoamerican flatbread made from corn or wheat.

tortilla de harina: Wheat flour tortilla.

Tortilla Wall: Term used for the fourteen-mile section of the U.S.-Mexico border fence that runs from the Otay Mesa border crossing in San Diego, California, to the Pacific Ocean.

tortillería: Tortilla-making shop that produces and sells freshly made tortillas.

Selected Bibliography

Aboites, A. Jaime. *Breve historia de un invento olvidado: Las máquinas tortilladoras en México.* Mexico City: Universidad Autónoma Metropolitana, 1989.

Acuña, Rodolfo. *Occupied America: A History of Chicanos.* Upper Saddle River, NJ: Pearson, 2010.

Alonzo, Armando. *Tejano Legacy: Rancheros and Settlers in South Texas, 1734–1900.* Albuquerque: University of New Mexico Press, 1998.

Alvarez, Maribel. "And Wheat Completed the Cycle: Flour Mills, Social Memory, and Industrial Culture in Sonora, Mexico." Lecture, Benjamin Botkin Lecture Series, American Folklife Center, Library of Congress. April 21, 2010.

American Institute of Baking (AIB) International. https://www.aibonline.org/resources/statistics/tortillas.html.

Arellano, Gustavo. *Taco USA: How Mexican Food Conquered America.* New York: Scribner, 2012.

Arreola, Daniel D. *Tejano South Texas: A Mexican American Cultural Province.* Austin: University of Texas Press, 2002.

Bacon, David. *Illegal People: How Globalization Creates Migration and Criminalizes Immigrants.* Boston, MA: Beacon Press, 2008.

———. "Taking on the Tortilla King." 1996. http://dbacon.igc.org/Strikes/06tortil.htm.

Baker, Lauren. *Corn Meets Maize: Food Movements and Markets in Mexico.* Lanham, MD: Rowman & Littlefield, 2012.

Baldwin, Debra Lee. *Taco Titan: The Glen Bell Story.* Arlington, TX: Summit Publishing Group, 1999.

Barros, Cristina, ed. *El Cocinero Mexicano: 1831.* Mexico City:

National Council for Culture and the Arts (Conaculta),
2000.

Bauer, Arnold. "Millers and Grinders: Technology and Household Economy in Mesoamerica." *Agricultural History* 64, no.
1 (Winter 1990): 1–17.

Bayless, Rick, and Deann Groen Bayless. *Authentic Mexican: Regional
Cooking from the Heart of Mexico*. New York: William Morrow
and Company, 1987.

Beck, Margaret. "Archaeological Signatures of Corn Preparation
in the U.S. Southwest." *KIVA* 67, no. 2 (2001): 187–218.

Beezley, William. *Judas at the Jockey Club and Other Episodes of Porfirian
Mexico*. Lincoln: University of Nebraska Press, 1987.

Benitez, A. M. de. *Cocina prehispánica*. Mexico City: Ediciónes
Euroamericas, 1976.

Berdan, Frances, and Patricia Anawalt. *The Essential Codex Mendoza*.
Berkeley: University of California Press, 1997.

Blanton, Richard E., Gary M. Feinman, Stephen A. Kowalewski,
and Linda M. Nicholas. *Ancient Oaxaca: The Monte Albán State*.
Cambridge: Cambridge University Press, 1999.

Blanton, Richard E., Stephen A. Kowalewski, Gary M. Feinman,
and Laura M. Finsten. *Ancient Mesoamerica: A Comparison of
Change in Three Regions*. Cambridge: Cambridge University
Press, 1993.

Booth, William. "Diana Kennedy, Fiery Chronicler of Mexican
Food Traditions." *Washington Post*. January 11, 2011.

Bravo, Joe. http://www.joebravo.net.

Calderón de la Barca, Frances, Howard Fisher, and Marion Hall
Fisher, eds. *Life in Mexico: The Letters of Fanny Calderón de la Barca*.
Garden City, NY: Doubleday, 1966.

Carmack, Robert, Janine Gasco, and Gary Gossen. *The Legacy of
Mesoamerica: History and Culture of a Native American Civilization*.
Upper Saddle River, NJ: Pearson, 2007.

Carrasco, David. *Daily Life of the Aztecs: People of the Sun and Earth*.
Westport, CT: Greenwood Press, 1998.

————, ed. *The Oxford Encyclopedia of Mesoamerican Cultures*. New York: Oxford University Press, 2001.

Castro, Rafaela. *Chicano Folklore: A Guide to the Folktales, Traditions, Rituals and Religious Practices of Mexican Americans*. Oxford: Oxford University Press, 2000.

Center for Foods of the Americas. New York: Culinary Institute of America. http://www.ciaprochef.com/CFA/.

Cheetham, David. "Corn, Colanders, and Cooking: Early Maize Processing in the Maya Lowlands and Its Implications." In *Pre-Columbian Foodways: Interdisciplinary Approaches to Food, Culture, and Markets in Ancient Mesoamerica*, edited by John Staller and David Carrasco, 325–68. New York: Springer, 2009.

Christie, Maria Elisa. *Kitchen Space: Women, Fiestas, and Everyday Life in Central Mexico*. Austin: University of Texas Press, 2008.

Coalition of Immokolee Workers. http://www.ciw-online.org.

Coe, Michael. *The Maya*. New York: Thames & Hudson, 2011.

Coe, Michael, and Rex Koontz. *Mexico: From the Olmecs to the Aztecs*. New York: Thames & Hudson, 2008.

Coe, Sophie. *America's First Cuisines*. Austin: University of Texas Press, 1994.

Cortés, Hernán. *Letters From Mexico*. Translated by Anthony Pagden. New Haven, CT: Yale University Press, 1986.

Counihan, Carole. *A Tortilla Is Like Life: Food and Culture in the San Luis Valley of Colorado*. Austin: University of Texas, 2010.

Counihan, Carole, and Penny Van Estenik. *Food and Culture: A Reader*. London: Routledge, 2012.

Cowen, Tyler. "Is Globalization Changing the Way the World Eats?" Address given at the International Association of Culinary Professionals. 26th Annual Conference, April 2004.

Cushing, Frank Hamilton. *Zuni Breadstuff*. New York: Museum of the American Indian, 1920.

DePalma, Anthony. "How a Tortilla Empire Was Built on Favoritism." *New York Times*, February 15, 1996.

Díaz del Castillo, Bernal. *The True History of the Conquest of New Spain.* Translated by Alfred Percival Maudslay. Surrey: Ashgate Publishing, 2010.

Dickerson, Marla. "Small Tortilla Makers Lose Anti-Trust Suit Against Rival." *Los Angeles Times,* January 6, 2004.

Dunn, Michael, Sergio O. Serna-Saldivar, Diana Sanchez-Hernandez, and Robert W. Griffin. "Commercial Evaluation of a Continuous Micronutrient Fortification Process for Nixtamal Tortillas." *Cereal Chemistry* 85, no. 6 (2008): 746–52.

Durán, Diego. *The Aztecs.* Translated by Doris Heyden and Fernando Horcasitas. New York: Orion Press, 1964.

Earle, Rebecca. *The Body of the Conquistador: Food, Race and the Colonial Experience in Spanish America, 1492–1700.* Cambridge: Cambridge University Press, 2012.

Eddy, F. W. *Metates and Manos: The Basic Corn Grinding Tools of the Southwest.* Santa Fe: Museum of New Mexico Press, 1979.

El maíz, fundamento de la cultura popular Mexicana. Mexico City: Museo Nacional de Culturas Populares, 1982.

Esteva, Gustavo, and Catherine Marielle. *Sin maíz no hay paíz.* Mexico City: National Council for Culture and the Arts (Conaculta), 2003.

Farb, Peter, and George Armelagas. *Consuming Passion: The Anthropology of Eating.* Boston, MA: Houghton Mifflin, 1980.

Feinman, Gary. "The Emergence of Specialized Ceramic Production in Formative Oaxaca." *Research in Economic Anthropology* Supplement 2 (1986): 347–73.

Feinman, Gary M., Richard A. Blanton, and Stephen A. Kowalewski. "Market System Development in the Prehispanic Valley of Oaxaca, Mexico." In *Trade and Exchange in Early Mesoamerica,* edited by Kenneth G. Hirth, 157–78. Albuquerque: University of New Mexico Press, 1984.

Fergusson, Edna. *Mexican Cookbook.* Albuquerque: University of New Mexico Press, 1945.

Fernández-Aceves, María Teresa. "Once We Were Corn Grinders: Women and Labor in the Tortilla Industry of Guadalajara, 1920–1940." *International Labor and Working Class History* 63 (Spring 2003): 81–101.

Ferry, Barbara, and Debbie Nathan. "Mistaken Identity? The Case of New Mexico's 'Hidden Jews.'" *Atlantic Monthly*, December 2000.

Flint, Richard, and Shirley Cushing Flint. *Documents of the Coronado Expedition, 1539–1542.* Dallas, TX: Southern Methodist University Press, 2005.

Foundation for the Advancement of Mesoamerican Studies (FAMSI). https://famsi.org.

Fowler-Salamini, Heather, and Mary Kay Vaughan. *Women of the Mexican Countryside, 1850–1990.* Tucson: University of Arizona Press, 1994.

Frank, Lois Ellen. *Foods of the Southwest Indian Nations: Traditional and Contemporary Native American Recipes.* Berkeley, CA: Ten Speed Press, 2002.

Fundación Herdez. http://www.fundacionherdez.com.mx /?p=pculturales.

Fussell, Betty. *The Story of Corn.* Albuquerque: University of New Mexico Press, 2004.

Gage, Thomas. *Thomas Gage's Travels in the New World.* Norman: University of Oklahoma Press, 1958.

Gibson, Charles. *The Aztecs Under Spanish Rule: A History of the Indians of the Valley of Mexico.* Stanford, CA: Stanford University Press, 1964.

———. *Spain in America.* New York: Harper & Row, 1966.

Gitlitz, David, and Linda Kay Davidson. *A Drizzle of Honey: The Lives and Recipes of Spain's Secret Jews.* New York: St. Martin's Press, 1999.

Grove, David C. *Ancient Chalcatzingo.* Austin: University of Texas Press, 1987.

———. "The Preclassic Societies of the Central Highlands of

Mesoamerica." In *Cambridge History of the Native Peoples of the Americas. Mesoamerica*, vol. II, edited by Richard E. W. Adam and Murdo J. MacLeod, 122–55. Cambridge: Cambridge University Press, 2000.

Gruma Corporation. *Sixty Years Gruma: The History That Nourishes Our Success*. Mexico City: Clio, 2009.

Guerrero Guerrero, Raúl. *Toneucáyotl: el pan nuestro de cada dia*. Mexico City: Instituto Nacional de Antropologia e Historia, 1987.

Guillermoprieto, Alma. "In Search of the Real Tortilla." *The New Yorker*, November 29, 1999. 46–48.

Hammond, George. *Coronado's Seven Cities*. Albuquerque, NM: United States Coronado Exposition Commission, 1940.

Hammond, George, and Agapito Rey. *Don Juan de Oñate, Colonizer of New Mexico: 1595–1628*. Albuquerque: University of New Mexico Press, 1953.

Haram, Karen. "The History of the Nacho." *San Antonio Express News*, March 26, 2006.

Hart, E. Richard. *Zuni and the Courts: A Struggle for Sovereign Land Rights*. Lawrence: University Press of Kansas, 1995.

Haury, Emil W. *Emil W. Haury's Prehistory of the American Southwest*. Edited by J. Jefferson Reid and David E. Doyel. Tucson: University of Arizona Press, 1986.

Hesser, Leon. *The Man Who Fed the World: Nobel Peace Prize Laureate Norman Borlaug and His Battle to End World Hunger*. Dallas, TX: Durban House, 2006.

Hicks, W. Whitney. "Agricultural Development in Northern Mexico, 1940–1960." *Land Economics* 43, no. 4 (November 1967): 393–402.

Jayasanker, Laresh Krishna. *Sameness in Diversity: Food Culture and Globalization in the San Francisco Bay Area and America, 1965–2005*. Ann Arbor, MI: ProQuest, 2008.

Jiménez, Alfredo, Nicolás Kanellos, and Claudio Esteva-Fabregat, eds. *Handbook of Hispanic Cultures in the United States*. Houston, TX: Arte Publico Press, 1994.

Jiménez, Jose Luis. "Border Fence into Pacific Ocean To Be Rebuilt." KPBS News, November 3, 2011.

Jinich, Pati. *Pati's Mexican Table: The Secret of Real Mexican Home Cooking.* Woodridge, IL: Houghton Mifflin Harcourt, 2013. http://www.patismexicantable.com.

Juárez Ramírez, Karina Jazmín. *Tortillas Ceremoniales.* Colección Arte y Culturas Populares de Guanajuato 4. Spanish text with translation to English by Paige Mitchell and to Otomí by Yolanda de Leon de Santiago. Guanajuato: Ediciones la Rana, 2010.

Katz, S. H., M. L. Hediger, and L. A. Valleroy. "Traditional Maize Processing Techniques in the New World." *Science* 184, no. 4138 (May 17, 1974): 765–73.

Kennedy, Diana. *The Cuisines of Mexico.* New York: Harper & Row, 1972.

———. *The Tortilla Book.* Revised ed. New York: HarperCollins, 1991.

Kennedy, Rory. *The Fence (Las Barda).* HBO Documentary, 2010.

Kessell, John. *Pueblos, Spaniards, and the Kingdom of New Mexico.* Norman: University of Oklahoma Press, 2010.

———. *Spain in the Southwest: A Narrative History of Colonial New Mexico, Arizona, Texas, and California.* Norman: University of Oklahoma Press, 2002.

Kingston, Michael. "The First Thanksgiving?" *Texas Almanac.* http://www.texasalmanac.com/topics/history/timeline/first-thanksgiving.

Kino, Eusebio Francisco. *Spain in the West: Kino's Historical Memoir of Pimería Alta.* Translated by Herbert Eugene Bolton. Cleveland, OH: A. H. Clark, 1919.

Kiple, Kenneth F., and Kriemhild Coneè Ornelas, eds. *The Cambridge World History of Food.* Cambridge: Cambridge University Press, 2000.

Landa, Diego. *The Maya: Diego de Landa's Account of the Affairs of Yucatan.* Translated by A. R. Pagden. Chicago, IL: J. P. O'Hara, 1975.

Lekson, Stephen. *A History of the Ancient Southwest.* Santa Fe, NM: School for Advanced Research Press, 2008.

Levenstein, Harvey. *Paradox of Plenty: A Social History of Eating in America.* Oxford: Oxford University Press, 1993.

Lewis, Oscar. *Five Families: Mexican Case Studies in the Culture of Poverty.* New York: Basic Books, 1959.

————. *Tepoztlán: Village in Mexico.* New York: Holt, Rinehart and Winston, 1960.

Lind, David, and Elizabeth Barham. "The Social Life of the Tortilla: Food, Cultural Politics, and Contested Commodification." *Agriculture and Human Values* 21 (2004): 47–60.

Livas, Eduardo, Jr. "Mexico Tortilla Maker Won No Favors." *New York Times,* February 21, 1996.

Long-Solís, Janet. *Conquista y comida: consecuencias del encuentro de dos mundos.* Mexico City: UNAM, Instituto de Investigaciones Historicas, 2003.

Long-Solís, Janet, and Luis Alberto Vargas. *Food Culture in Mexico.* Westport, CT: Greenwood Press, 2005.

MacClancy, Jeremy. *Consuming Culture: Why You Eat What You Eat.* New York: Henry Holt, 1992.

MacLachlan, Colin, and William Beezley. *El Gran Pueblo: A History of Greater Mexico.* Englewood Cliffs, NJ: Prentice Hall, 1994.

Martínez, Oscar. *Mexican Origin People in the United States: A Topical History.* Tucson: University of Arizona Press, 2001.

The Meaning of Food. Pie in the Sky Productions in association with Oregon Public Broadcasting. 2005. http://pbs.org/opb /meaningoffood.

Miller, Simon. "Wheat Production in Europe and America: Mexican Problems in Comparative Perspective, 1770–1910." *Agricultural History* 68, no. 3 (Summer 1994): 16–34.

Mills, Barbara. "How the Pueblos Became Global: Colonial Appropriations, Resistance, and Diversity in the North American Southwest." *Archaeologies: Journal of the World Archaeological Congress* 4, no. 2 (2008): 218-32.

————, ed. *Identity, Feasting, and the Archaeology of the Greater Southwest.*
Boulder: University Press of Colorado, 2004.

Ministry of Economy, Department of Basic Industries. *Analysis of
the Corn Tortilla Value Chain: Current Situation and Local Corn Competition Factors.* www.economia.gob.mx. 2011.

Minnis, Paul, ed. *People and Plants in Ancient Western North America.*
Tucson: University of Arizona Press, 2004.

Minsa Corn Flour. "60 Years of Experience." http://www
.minsa.com

Monaghan, John. *The Covenants with Earth and Rain: Exchange, Sacrifice,
and Revelation in Mixtec Sociality.* Norman: University of Oklahoma Press, 1995.

Muñon, Domingo Francisco de San Antón Chimalpahin
Quauhtlehuanitzin. *Exercicio quotidiano.* In *Codex Chimalpahin.*
Vol. 2, *Society and Politics in Mexico Tenochtitlan, Tlatelolco, Texcoco,
Culhuacan, and Other Nahua Altepetl in Central Mexico.* Translated
by Arthur J. O. Anderson and Susan Schroeder. Norman:
University of Oklahoma Press, 1997.

Muñoz, Caroline Bank. *Transnational Tortillas: Race, Gender, and Shop
Floor Politics in Mexico and the United States.* Ithaca, NY: ILR
Press, 2008.

Myers, Sandra, ed. *Ho for California! Women's Overland Diaries.* San
Marino, CA: Huntington Library, 1980.

Nabhan, Gary Paul. *The Desert Smells Like Rain: A Naturalist in Papago
Indian Country.* San Francisco, CA: North Point Press, 1982.

National Institute of Anthropology and History (INAH). Mexico. http://www.inah.gob.mx.

Navarro, Carlos. "Tortilla Consumption Continues to Decline
in Mexico but Grows Steadily Overseas." *SourceMex Economic
News and Analysis on Mexico,* June 23, 2004.

Nickerson, Michelle, and Darren Dochuk. *Sunbelt Rising: The Politics
of Place, Space, and Region.* Philadelphia: University of Pennsylvania Press, 2011.

Niethammer, Carolyn. *American Indian Food and Lore.* New York:
Collier, 1974.

Ochoa, Enrique. *Feeding Mexico: The Political Uses of Food since 1910.* Wilmington, DE: Scholarly Resources, 2000.

Pew Hispanic Center. http://www.pewhispanic.org.

Pfefferkorn, Ignaz. *Sonora: A Description of the Province.* Translated by Theodore Treutlein. Tucson: University of Arizona Press, 1989.

Pilcher, Jeffrey M. *Planet Taco: A Global History of Mexican Food.* Oxford: Oxford University Press, 2012.

————. *¡Que vivan los tamales!: Food and the Making of Mexican Identity.* Albuquerque: University of New Mexico Press, 1998.

Pitt, Leonard. *The Decline of the Californios: A Social History of the Spanish-Speaking Californians, 1846–1890.* Berkeley: University of California Press. 1966.

Pohl, John. "The Meeting: Two Points of View." *John Pohl's Meso-america.* Foundation for the Advancement of Mesoamerican Studies (FAMSI). http://.famsi.org/research/pohl/pohl_meeting.html.

Pueblo de maíz: La cocina ancestral de México. Mexico City: National Council for Culture and the Arts (Conaculta), 2004.

Rea, Amadeo. *At the Desert's Green Edge: An Ethnobotany of the Gila River Pima.* Tucson: University of Arizona Press, 1997.

Reed, John. *Insurgent Mexico.* New York: D. Appleton, 1914.

Reyes, José Hernández, ed. *People of Corn: Mexico's Ancestral Cuisine.* Mexico City: National Council for Culture and the Arts (Conaculta), 2004.

Ríos, Kristofer. "After Long Fight, Farmworkers in Florida Win an Increase in Pay." *New York Times,* January 18, 2011.

Robbins, Ted. "San Diego Fence Provides Lessons in Border Control." National Public Radio, April 6, 2006.

Roig-Franzia, Manuel. "A Culinary and Cultural Staple in Crisis." *Washington Post,* January 27, 2007.

Rooney, Lloyd W., Ricardo Bressani, and Sergio O. Serna-Saldivar. "Fortification of Corn Masa Flour with Iron and /or Other Nutrients: A Literature and Industry Experience Review." *SUSTAIN,* December 1997.

Sahagún, Bernardino de, *General History of the Things of New Spain: Florentine Codex.* Translated by C. E. Dibble and A. J. O. Anderson. Santa Fe, NM: School of American Research, 1950–82.

Salas, Elizabeth. *Soldaderas in the Mexican Military: Myth and History.* Austin: University of Texas Press, 1990.

Sandstrom, Alan R. *Corn Is in Our Blood: Culture and Ethnic Identity in a Contemporary Aztec Indian Village.* Lexington: University of Kentucky Press, 1991.

Sandstrom, Alan R., and Pamela Effrein Sandstrom. *Traditional Papermaking and Paper Cult Figures of Mexico.* Norman: University of Oklahoma Press, 1986.

Schlissel, Lillian, Byrd Gibbens, and Elizabeth Hampsten. *Far From Home: Families of the Westward Journey.* Lincoln: University of Nebraska Press, 1989.

Serna-Saldivar, Sergio O. "Research Developments in the Science, Technology and Nutritional Value of Maize-Based Nixtamalized Foods." In *The ICC Book of Ethnic Cereal-Based Foods Across the Continents,* edited by J.Taylor and R. Cracknell, 133–63. Pretoria, South Africa: University of Pretoria, 2009.

Seymour, Deni. *Where the Earth and Sky Are Sewn Together: Sobaipuri-O'odham Contexts of Contact and Colonialism.* Salt Lake City: University of Utah Press, 2011.

Smith, Andrew, ed. *The Oxford Companion to American Food and Drink.* New York: Oxford University Press, 2007.

Snow, David. "Tener Comal y Metate: Protohistoric Rio Grande Maize Use and Diet." In *Perspectives on Southwestern Prehistory,* edited by Paul E. Minnis and Charles L. Redman, 289–300. Boulder, CO: Westview, 1990.

Sokolov, Raymond. *Why We Eat What We Eat: How the Encounter Between the New World and the Old Changed the Way Everyone Eats.* New York: Summit Books, 1991.

Sonnichsen, C. L. "Salt War of San Elizario." *Handbook of Texas Online.* Texas State Historical Association. June 15, 2010.

http://www.tshaonline.org/handbook/online/articles
/jcs01.

Spicer, Edward. *Cycles of Conquest: The Impact of Spain, Mexico, and the
United States on the Indians of the Southwest, 1533–1960.* Tucson:
University of Arizona Press, 1962.

Staller, John, and Michael Carrasco. *Pre-Columbian Foodways:
Interdisciplinary Approaches to Food, Culture and Markets in Ancient
Mesoamerica.* New York: Springer, 2009.

Stevenson, Mark. "What's Eating Mexico? Declining Torta
Sales." *San Diego Union-Tribune,* July 25, 2004.

The Storm That Swept Mexico. Directed by Raymond Telles.
Paradigm Productions in association with Public Broadcasting Service (PBS). 2011. http://www.pbs.org/itvs
/storm-that-swept-mexico.

Strehl, Dan, trans. and ed. *Encarnación's Kitchen: Mexican Recipes from
Nineteenth-Century California. Selections from Encarnación Pinedo's El
Cocinero Español.* Berkeley: University of California Press,
2003.

Super, John. *Food, Conquest, and Colonization in Sixteenth-Century Spanish
America.* Albuquerque: University of New Mexico Press,
1988.

SUSTAIN. *Storage, Sensory, and Bioavailability Evaluation of Iron Fortified
Corn Masa Flour.* August 2000. http://www.sustaintech.org.

Taube, Karl. *Aztec and Maya Myths.* Austin: University of Texas
Press, 1993.

———. "The Maize Tamale in Classic Maya Diet, Epigraphy,
and Art." *American Antiquity* 54 (1989): 31–51.

Tausend, Marilyn. *Savoring Mexico.* San Francisco: Williams-
Sonoma, 2001.

Tedlock, Dennis, trans. *Popol Vuh: The Definitive Edition of the Mayan
Book of the Dawn of Life and the Glories of Gods and Kings.* New
York: Simon and Schuster, 1996.

Thomas, Hugh. *Conquest: Cortes, Montezuma, and the Fall of Old Mexico.*
New York: Simon and Schuster, 1995.

Tinker Salas, Miguel. *In the Shadow of the Eagles: Sonora and the Transformation of the Border during the Porfiriato.* Berkeley: University of California Press, 1997.

Tortilla Industry of America (TIA). http://www.tortilla-info .com.

Trans-Border Institute (TBI). University of San Diego. San Diego, CA. http://www.sandiego.edu/peace studies /institutes/tbi.

Treutlein, Theodore. "The Economic Regime of the Jesuit Missions in Eighteenth Century Sonora." *Pacific Historical Review* 8, no. 3 (September 1939): 289–300.

Valle, Victory. "A Curse of Tea and Potatoes." In *Encarnación's Kitchen: Mexican Recipes from Nineteenth-Century California.* Selections from *Encarnación Pinedo's* El Cocinero Español, edited and translated by Dan Strehl, 1–18. Berkeley: University of California Press, 2003.

Vélez-Ibáñez, Carlos. *Border Visions: Mexican Culture of the Southwest United States.* Tucson: University of Arizona Press, 1996.

Vogt, Evon. *Tortillas for the Gods: A Symbolic Analysis of Zinacanteco Rituals.* Cambridge, MA: Harvard University Press, 1976.

Walch, Tad. "BYU Team Builds a Better Tortilla." *Deseret News,* December 1, 2008.

Warman, Arturo. *Corn & Capitalism: How a Botanical Bastard Grew to Global Dominance.* Translated by Nancy Westrate. Chapel Hill: University of North Carolina Press, 2007.

Waters, Frank. *Book of the Hopi.* New York: Penguin, 1977.

West, Robert. *Sonora: Its Geographical Personality.* Austin: University of Texas Press, 2009.

Womack, John, Jr. *Zapata and the Mexican Revolution.* New York: Random House, 2011.

Yetman, David. *Conflict in Colonial Sonora: Indians, Priests and Settlers.* Albuquerque: University of New Mexico Press, 2012.

Index